COLLINS GEM

FACT FILE

**Elaine Henderson
William Allan**

KU-033-340

TED SMART

This edition produced for The Book People Ltd,
Hall Wood Avenue, Haydock, St Helens WA11 9UL

HarperCollins Publishers
Westerhill Road, Bishopbriggs, Glasgow G64 2QT

First Published 1994
Updated, 1995, 1996, 1997, 1998, 1999, 2000
This edition published 2002

Reprint 10 9 8 7 6 5 4 3 2 1

© HarperCollins Publishers 2002

ISBN 0 00 765939 3

All rights reserved, Collins Gem® is a registered trademark
of HarperCollins Publishers Limited

Layout and design by
Bounford.com
5 The Malting, Green Drift, Royston, Herts SG8 5D7

Printed in Germany by Elsnerdruck, Berlin

Foreword

Have you ever tried to find the answer to what you originally thought was a relatively simple question? Have you ever searched high and low and finally given up in complete exasperation? The *Gem Fact File* is the book you need, with its thousands of difficult-to-remember and hard-to-find facts. Here you will find the answers to such diverse enquiries as 'What are the member countries of NATO?' and 'Who were the Seven Fathers of the Church?' There are lists of everything from phobias, chemical elements, winners of the Booker Prize and Olympic Games venues, to the world's five largest deserts, the seven liberal arts and the winners of the championships in all the major sports. In among the hard facts are entries on more lighthearted matters, such as the order of the presents in the song 'The Twelve Days of Christmas'.

This fascinating little book draws together material from nine distinct fields: Politics, History, Geography, Religion, Science, The Arts, Language, Sport and General Interest.

Like its numerical companion volume, *Gem Ready Reference*, the *Gem Fact File* provides an easy-to-use quick reference point for a broad miscellany of information that could only be otherwise obtained after consulting a wide variety of sources, and as such will appeal to everyone from trivia buffs and quiz compilers to students and journalists.

Contents

Politics

History

Geography

Religion

Languages

Sport

Politics

COUNTRIES OF THE WORLD

Country	Area	Principal Language(s)
Afghanistan	Asia	Dari; Pushtu
Albania	Europe	Albanian; Greek
Algeria	Africa	Arabic; Berber; French
Andorra	Europe	Catalan; French; Spanish
Angola	Africa	Portuguese; Bantu
Anguilla (UK)	C America	English
Antigua & Barbuda	C America	English
Argentina	S America	Spanish
Armenia	Europe	Armenian
Aruba (Neth)	C America	Dutch; Papiamento; Spanish
Australia	Oceania	English
Austria	Europe	German; Croatian; Slovene
Azerbaijan	Europe	Azeri; Russian
Bahamas	C America	English
Bahrain	Asia	Arabic; Farsi; Urdu; English
Bangladesh	Asia	Bengali
Barbados	C America	English
Belarus	Europe	Belorussian; Russian
Belgium	Europe	Flemish/Dutch; French; German
Belize	C America	English; Spanish; Garifunga; Maya
Benin	Africa	French; Fon; Adja
Bermuda (UK)	C America	English

Currency	Capital	Intl. Car Reg
Afghani	Kabul	AFG
Lek	Tirana	AL
Dinar	Algiers	DZ
Franc; Peseta	Andorra la Vella	AND
Kwanza	Luanda	–
E Caribbean $	The Valley	–
E Caribbean $	St John's	–
Argentine Peso	Buenos Aires	RA
Dram	Yerevan	–
Florin	Oranjestad	–
Australian $	Canberra	AUS
Euro	Vienna	A
Manat	Baku	–
Bahamian $	Nassau	BS
Dinar	Manama	BRN
Taka	Dhaka	BD
Barbados $	Bridgetown	BDS
Rouble	Minsk	BER*
Euro	Brussels	B
Belizean $	Belmopan	BH
CFA Franc	Porto Novo	DY
Bermuda $	Hamilton	–

Country	Area	Principal Language(s)
Bhutan	Asia	Dzongkha; Nepalese
Bolivia	S America	Spanish; Quechua; Aymará
Bosnia-Herzegovina	Europe	Serbian; Croatian; Bosnian
Botswana	Africa	English; Tswana
Brazil	S America	Portuguese; Indian languages
Brunei	Asia	Malay; English
Bulgaria	Europe	Bulgarian; Turkish
Burkina Faso	Africa	French; Moré; African languages
Burundi	Africa	French; Kirundi; Swahili
Cambodia	Asia	Khmer; French
Cameroon	Africa	French; English; African languages
Canada	N America	English; French; Indian and Inuit
Cape Verde	Africa	Portuguese; Criolo
Cayman Islands (UK)	C America	English
Central African Rep.	Africa	French; Sangho
Chad	Africa	Arabic; French; African languages
Chile	S America	Spanish
China	Asia	Standard Chinese; Cantonese and other dialects
Colombia	S America	Spanish
Comoros	Africa	Arabic; French; Kiswahili
Congo, Rep. of	Africa	French; African languages
Congo, Dem. Rep. of	Africa	French; English; Bantu
Costa Rica	C America	Spanish
Côte d'Ivoire	Africa	French; Akan; Kru
Croatia	Europe	Croatian

Currency	Capital	Intl. Car Reg
Ngultrum	Thimphu	–
Boliviano	La Paz/Sucre	–
Dinar	Sarajevo	–
Pula	Gaborone	RB
Real	Brasilia	BR
Brunei $	Bandar Seri Begawan	BRU
Lev	Sofia	BG
CFA Franc	Ougadougou	–
Burundi Franc	Bujumbura	RU
Riel	Phnom Penh	K
CFA Franc	Yaoundé	–
Canadian $	Ottawa	CDN
Cape Verde Escudo	Praia	–
Cayman Islands $	George Town	–
CFA Franc	Bangui	RCA
CFA Franc	N'djamena	–
Peso	Santiago	RCH
Yuan	Beijing	–
Peso	Bogotá	CO
Comoran Franc	Moroni	–
CFA Franc	Brazzaville	RCB
New Zaire	Kinshasa	ZRE
Colon	San José	CR
CFA Franc	Yamoussoukro	CI
Kuna	Zagreb	CRO*

Country	Area	Principal Language(s)
Cuba	C America	Spanish
Cyprus	Europe	Greek; Turkish
Czech Republic	Europe	Czech; Hungarian; Slovak
Denmark	Europe	Danish
Djibouti	Africa	Arabic
Dominica	C America	English; French
Dominican Republic	C America	Spanish
East Timor	Asia	Portugese, Tetum
Ecuador	S America	Spanish; Quechua
Egypt	Africa	Arabic
El Salvador	C America	Spanish
Equatorial Guinea	Africa	Spanish
Eritrea	Africa	English; Arabic
Estonia	Europe	Estonian; Russian
Ethiopia	Africa	Amharic
Falkland Islands (UK)	S America	English
Faroe Islands	Europe	Faroese; Danish
Fiji	Oceania	English; Fijian
Finland	Europe	Finnish; Swedish; Saam
France	Europe	French
French Guiana	S America	French
Gabon	Africa	French; Bantu
Gambia	Africa	English; Wolof; Mandinka; Fula
Georgia	Europe	Georgian; Russian
Germany	Europe	German
Ghana	Africa	English; Akan; Ewe; Ga
Gibraltar (UK)	Europe	English; Spanish

Currency	Capital	Intl. Car Reg
Peso	Havana	C
Cypriot £	Nicosia (Lefkosia)	CY
Koruna	Prague	CS
Krone	Copenhagen	DK
Djibouti Franc	Djibouti	–
E Caribbean $	Roseau	WD
Peso	Santo Domingo	DOM
US$	Dili	
Sucre	Quito	EC
Egyptian £	Cairo	ET
Colón	San Salvador	ES
CFA Franc	Malabo	–
Ethiopian birr	Asmara	–
Kroon	Tallinn	EW*
Birr	Addis Ababa	ETH
Falkland £	Port Stanley	–
Danish Krone	Tórshavn	FR
Fiji $	Suva	FJI
Euro	Helsinki	SF
Euro	Paris	F
Euro	Cayenne	F
CFA Franc	Libreville	–
Dalasi	Banjul	WAG
Lari	Tbilisi	GRU*
Euro	Berlin	D
Cedi	Accra	GH
Gibraltar £	Gibraltar	GBZ

Country	Area	Principal Language(s)
Greece	Europe	Greek
Greenland (Den)	N America	Danish; Inuit
Grenada	C America	English; French patois
Guadeloupe (Fr)	C America	French
Guam (US)	Oceania	Chamorro; English; Japanese
Guatemala	C America	Spanish; Indian dialects
Guinea	Africa	French; African languages
Guinea-Bissau	Africa	Portuguese; Criolo; Balante
Guyana	S America	English; Hindi; Urdu
Haiti	C America	French; Creole French
Honduras	C America	Spanish; Indian dialects
Hungary	Europe	Hungarian
Iceland	Europe	Icelandic
India	Asia	Hindi; English; Indian languages
Indonesia	Asia	Bahasa Indonesian; English; Dutch
Iran	Asia	Farsi (Persian)
Iraq	Asia	Arabic; English; Kurdish
Ireland, Rep. of	Europe	English; Irish Gaelic
Israel	Asia	Hebrew; Arabic
Italy	Europe	Italian
Jamaica	C America	English; Jamaican creole
Japan	Asia	Japanese
Jordan	Asia	Arabic
Kazakstan	Asia	Kazakh; Russian; German
Kenya	Africa	Swahili; English

Currency	Capital	Intl. Car Reg
Euro	Athens	GR
Danish Krone	Nuuk (Godthåb)	–
E Caribbean $	St George's	WG
Euro	Basse Terre	F
US $	Agaña	–
Quetzal	Guatemala City	GCA
Guinean Guilder	Conakry	–
Peso	Bissau	–
Guyana $	Georgetown	GUY
Gourde	Port-au-Prince	RH
Lempira	Tegucigalpa	–
Forint	Budapest	H
Króna	Reykjavik	IS
Rupee	New Delhi	IND
Rupiah	Jakarta	RI
Rial	Teheran	IR
Dinar	Baghdad	IRQ
Euro	Dublin	IRL
New Israeli Shekel	Jerusalem	IL
Euro	Rome	I
Jamaican $	Kingston	JA
Yen	Tokyo	J
Dinar	Amman	HKJ
Tenge	Astana	–
Kenya Shilling	Nairobi	EAK

Akmola from 2000

Country	Area	Principal Language(s)
Kiribati	Oceania	English; Gilbertese
Korea, People's Dem. Rep. of North	Asia	Korean
Korea, Rep. of South	Asia	Korean
Kuwait	Asia	Arabic
Kyrgyzstan	Asia	Russian; Kyrgyz
Laos	Asia	Lao; French; indigenous languages
Latvia	Europe	Latvian
Lebanon	Asia	Arabic; French; English; Armenian
Lesotho	Africa	Sesotho; English
Liberia	Africa	English; Niger-Congo languages
Libya	Africa	Arabic; English; French
Liechtenstein	Europe	German
Lithuania	Europe	Lithuanian
Luxembourg	Europe	French; German; Letzeburgesch
Macao (Port)	Asia	Portuguese; Chinese (Cantonese); English
Macedonia	Europe	Macedonian
Madagascar	Africa	Malagasy; French
Malawi	Africa	English; Chichewa
Malaysia	Asia	Malay; Chinese; English; Tamil
Maldives	Asia	Divehi; Arabic; Hindi; English
Mali	Africa	French; Bambara
Malta	Europe	Maltese; English
Mariana Islands, Northern (US)	Oceania	English; Chamoro

Currency	Capital	Intl. Car Reg
Australian $	Bairiki	–
Won	Pyongyang	–
Won	Seoul	ROK
Dinar	Kuwait City	KWT
Som	Bishkek	–
Kip	Vientiane	LAO
Lats	Riga	LR*
Lebanese £	Beirut	RL
Loti	Maseru	LS
Liberian $	Monrovia	LB
Dinar	Tripoli	LAR
Swiss Franc	Vaduz	FL
Litas	Vilnius	LT
Euro	Luxembourg	L
Pataca	Nome de Deus de Macau	–
Denar	Skopje	–
Malagasy Franc	Antananarivo	RM
Kwacha	Lilongwe	MW
Ringgit	Kuala Lumpur	MAL
Rufiyaa	Malé	–
CFA Franc	Bamako	RMM
Lira	Valletta	M
US $	Saipan	–

Country	Area	Principal Language(s)
Marshall Islands	Oceania	Marshallese; English; Japanese
Martinique (Fr)	C America	French
Mauritania	Africa	Arabic; French
Mauritius	Africa	English; Creole French
Mayotte (Fr)	Africa	French
Mexico	N America	Spanish; indigenous languages
Micronesia, Fed. States of	Oceania	English; several indigenous languages
Moldova	Europe	Moldavian
Monaco	Europe	French; English; Italian; Monegasque
Mongolia	Asia	Khalkha; Chinese; Russian
Montserrat (UK)	C America	English
Morocco	Africa	Arabic; Berber; French; Spanish
Mozambique	Africa	Portuguese; Swahili; Bantu
Myanmar (Burma)	Asia	Burmese; indigenous languages
Namibia	Africa	English; Afrikaans; German
Nauru	Oceania	Nauruan; English
Nepal	Asia	Nepali; Maithir; Bhojpuri
Netherlands	Europe	Dutch
Netherlands Antilles (Neth)	C America	Dutch; Papiamento; English; Spanish
New Caledonia (Fr)	Oceania	French; Melanesian-Polynesian dialects
New Zealand	Oceania	English; Maori
Nicaragua	C America	Spanish; Indian; English
Niger	Africa	French; Hausa; Songhai
Nigeria	Africa	English; Hausa; Ibo; Yoruba

Currency	Capital	Intl. Car Reg
US $	Dalap-Vliga-Darrit	–
Euro	Fort-de-France	F
Ouguiya	Nouakchott	RIM
Rupee	Port Louis	MS
Euro	Dzaoudzi	F
Peso	Mexico City	MEX
US $	Palikir	–
Leu	Chisinau	MOL*
Franc	Monaco-Ville	MC
Tugrik	Ulaanbaatar	–
E Caribbean $	Plymouth	–
Dirham	Rabat	MA
Metical	Maputo	–
Kyat	Yangon	BUR
Namibian $	Windhoek	SWA
Australian $	Yaren District	–
Rupee	Kathmandu	–
Euro	Amsterdam	NL
NL Antillian Guilder Aruba	Willemstad	NA
CFP Franc	Nouméa	F
New Zealand $	Wellington	NZ
Córdobaoro	Managua	NIC
CFA Franc	Niamey	RN
Naira	Abuja	WAN

Country	Area	Principal Language(s)
Norway	Europe	Norwegian; Lapp; Finnish
Oman	Asia	Arabic; English; Mahri languages
Pakistan	Asia	Urdu; English; Punjabi; Sindhi; Pashto; Baluchi; Brahvi
Palau	Oceania	Palauan; English
Panama	C America	Spanish; English; indigenous languages
Papua New Guinea	Oceania	Pidgin English; Motu; indigenous languages
Paraguay	S America	Spanish; Guaraní
Peru	S America	Spanish; Quechua; Aymará
Philippines	Asia	Tagalog; English; indigenous languages
Pitcairn Islands (UK)	Oceania	English
Poland	Europe	Polish
Polynesia, French	Oceania	French; Tahitian
Portugal	Europe	Portuguese
Puerto Rico (US)	C America	Spanish; English
Qatar	Asia	Arabic; English
Réunion (Fr)	Africa	French
Romania	Europe	Romanian; French; Hungarian; German
Russia	Europe	Russian; indigenous languages
Rwanda	Africa	French; Kinyarwanda; English
St Christopher (Kitts) & Nevis	C America	English; Creole English
St Helena (UK)	Africa	English
St Lucia	C America	English; French patois

Currency	Capital	Intl. Car Reg
Krone	Oslo	N
Rial Omani	Muscat	–
Rupee	Islamabad	PAK
US $	Koror	–
Balboa	Panama City	PA
Kina	Port Moresby	PNG
Guaraní	Asunción	PY
New Sol	Lima	PE
Peso	Manila	RP
NZ $	Adamstown	–
Zloty	Warsaw	PL
CFP Franc	Papeete	F
Euro	Lisbon	P
US $	San Juan	–
Riyal	Doha	–
Euro	St Denis	F
Leu	Bucharest	RO
Rouble	Moscow	RUS*
Rwanda Franc	Kigali	RWA
E Caribbean $	Basseterre	–
St Helena £	Jamestown	–
E Caribbean $	Castries	WL

Country	Area	Principal Language(s)
St Pierre & Miquelon (Fr)	N America	French
St Vincent & the Grenadines	C America	English; French patois
Samoa, American	Oceania	English; Samoan
San Marino	Europe	Italian
São Tomé & Príncipe	Africa	Portuguese; Creolo languages
Saudi Arabia	Asia	Arabic
Senegal	Africa	French; indigenous languages
Seychelles	Africa	English; Creole French; English
Sierra Leone	Africa	English; Krio
Singapore	Asia	English; Malay; Chinese; Tamil
Slovakia	Europe	Slovak; Czech; Hungarian
Slovenia	Europe	Slovene; Croatian
Solomon Islands	Oceania	English; indigenous languages
Somalia	Africa	Somali; Arabic
South Africa	Africa	Afrikaans; English; indigenous languages
Spain	Europe	Spanish; Catalan; Galician; Basque
Sri Lanka	Asia	Sinhala; Tamil
Sudan	Africa	Arabic; indigenous languages
Suriname	S America	Dutch; Hindi; Javanese
Swaziland	Africa	English; Swazi
Sweden	Europe	Swedish; Finnish; Saami
Switzerland	Europe	German; French; Italian; Romansch
Syria	Asia	Arabic; Kurdish; Armenian

Currency	Capital	Intl. Car Reg
Franc	St Pierre	F
E Caribbean $	Kingstown	WV
US $	Fagatogo	–
Lira	San Marino	RSM
Dobra	São Tomé	–
Riyal	Riyadh	–
CFA Franc	Dakar	SN
Rupee	Victoria	SY
Leone	Freetown	WAL
Singapore $	Singapore City	SGP
Koruna	Bratislava	SQ*
Tolar	Ljubljana	SLO*
Solomon Islands $	Honiara	–
Somali Shilling	Mogadishu	–
Rand	Cape Town/Pretoria	ZA
Euro	Madrid	E
Rupee	Sri Jayawardenapura/Colombo	CL
Sudanese dinar	Khartoum	–
Suriname Guilder	Paramaribo	SME
Lilangeni	Mbabane	SD
Krona	Stockholm	S
Swiss Franc	Bern	CH
Syrian £	Damascus	SYR

Country	Area	Principal Language(s)
Taiwan	Asia	Mandarin; Taiwanese; Hakka
Tajikistan	Asia	Tajik; Russian
Tanzania	Africa	Swahili; English
Thailand	Asia	Thai; Malay; English
Togo	Africa	French; Ewe
Tonga	Oceania	Tongan; English
Trinidad & Tobago	C America	English; Hindi; French; Spanish
Tunisia	Africa	Arabic; French; Berber
Turkey	Asia	Turkish; Kurdish; Arabic
Turkmenistan	Asia	Turkmenian; Russian; Uzbek
Turks & Caicos Islands (UK)	C America	English
Tuvalu	Oceania	Tuvaluan; English
Uganda	Africa	English; Swahili; Luganda; Luo; Ateso
Ukraine	Europe	Ukrainian; Russian
United Arab Emirates	Asia	Arabic; Farsi; Hindi; Urdu; English
United Kingdom	Europe	English; Irish and Scots Gaelic; Welsh
United States of America	N America	English; Spanish
Uruguay	S America	Spanish
Uzbekistan	Asia	Uzbek
Vanuatu	Oceania	Bislama; English; French
Vatican City	Europe	Italian; Latin
Venezuela	S America	Spanish; indigenous languages; Italian
Vietnam	Asia	Vietnamese; French; English; Khmer; Chinese

Currency	Capital	Intl. Car Reg
Taiwan $	Taibei	RC
Rouble	Dunshanbe	–
Tanzanian Shilling	Dodoma	EAZ
Baht	Bangkok	T
CFA Franc	Lomé	TG
Pa'anga	Nuku'alofa	–
Trinidad & Tobago $	Port of Spain	TT
Dinar	Tunis	TN
Lira	Ankara	TR
Manat	Ashkhabad	–
US $	Cockburn Town	–
Australian $	Funafuti	–
Uganda Shilling	Kampala	EAU
Hryvr	Kiev	UKR*
Dirham	Abu Dhabi	–
£ Sterling	London	GB
US $	Washington DC	USA
New Uruguayan Peso	Montevideo	ROU
Sum	Tashkent	–
Vatu	Port Vila	–
Lira	Vatican City	V
Bolívar	Caracas	YV
Dông	Hanoi	VN

Country	Area	Principal Language(s)
Virgin Islands (UK)	C America	English; Spanish; Creole
Virgin Islands (US)	C America	English; Spanish; Creole
Wallis & Futuna Islands (Fr)	Oceania	French; indigenous languages
Western Samoa	Oceania	Samoan; English
Yemen	Asia	Arabic; English
Yugoslavia, Fed. Rep. of	Europe	Serbian; Albanian; Hungarian
Zambia	Africa	English; Bantu; indigenous languages
Zimbabwe	Africa	English; Shona; Ndebele

Registration in use but not yet officially established.
No internationally-recognized registration letters have yet been allocated to states of the former USSR and Yugoslavia.

Currency	Capital	Intl. Car Reg
US $	Road Town	–
US $	Charlotte Amalie	–
CFP Franc	Mata-Utu	F
Tala	Apia	WS
Riyal	Sana/Aden	–
Dinar	Belgrade	YU
Kwacha	Lusaka	Z
Zimbabwe $	Harare	ZW

MAJOR POLITICAL GROUPINGS

Arab League

Founded in 1945 to promote Arab unity.

Members (original members in italics)

Algeria	*Jordan*	Oman	Sudan
Bahrain	Kuwait	Palestine	*Syria*
Comoros	*Lebanon*	PLO	Tunisia
Djibouti	Libya	Qatar	UAE
Egypt	Mauritania	*Saudi Arabia*	*Yemen*
Iraq	Morocco	Somalia	

Andean Group (Grupo Andino)

South American organization founded in 1969 for economic and social cooperation between members.

Members (original members in italics)

Bolivia	*Colombia*	*Ecuador*	*Peru*	Venezuela

Chile withdrew in 1977.

APEC (Asia Pacific Economic Cooperation)

Initiated in November 1989 as an informal consultative forum to promote multilateral economic cooperation on issues of trade and development.

Members

Australia	Japan	Philippines
Brunei	Malaysia	Republic of Korea
Canada	Mexico	Singapore
Chile	New Zealand	Taiwan*
China	Papua New	Thailand
Indonesia	Guinea	USA

Admitted as Chinese Taipei; Peru, Russia and Vietnam from 1998.

CARICOM (Caribbean Community and Common Market)

Established in 1973 by the Treaty of Chaguaramas for foreign policy and economic and social coordination in the Caribbean region.

Members

Antigua & Barbuda	Jamaica
Bahamas*	Montserrat
Barbados	St Christopher & Nevis
Belize	St Lucia
British Virgin Islands‡	St Vincent & the Grenadines
Dominica	Suriname
Grenada	Trinidad & Tobago
Guyana	Turks & Caicos Islands‡

Bahamas is a member of the Community but not of the Common Market.
‡ *Associate member*

Observer status

Dominican Rep.	Mexico	Venezuela
Haiti	Puerto Rico	

The Commonwealth

An informal association of sovereign states, without charter or constitution but coordinated by the Commonwealth Secretariat in London. Inaugurated in 1926 and based originally on membership of the British Empire. It is now a multi-racial association of equal, independent nations.

Members (and date of joining)

Antigua & Barbuda (1981)	Guyana (1966)
Australia (1931)	India (1947)
Bahamas (1973)	Jamaica (1962)
Bangladesh (1972)	Kenya (1963)
Barbados (1966)	Kiribati (1979)
Belize (1981)	Lesotho (1966)
Botswana (1966)	Malawi (1964)
Brunei (1984)	Malaysia (1957)
Cameroon (1995)	Maldives (1982)
Canada (1931)	Malta (1964)
Cyprus (1961)	Mauritius (1968)
Dominica (1978)	Mozambique (1995)
Gambia, The (1965)	Namibia (1990)
Ghana (1957)	Nauru (1968)
Grenada (1974)	New Zealand (1931)

Members (and date of joining) *cont.*

Nigeria (1960)*

Pakistan (1947; left 1972; rejoined 1989)

Papua New Guinea (1975)

St Christopher & Nevis (1983)

St Lucia (1979)

St Vincent & the Grenadines (1979)

Seychelles (1976)

Sierra Leone (1961)

Singapore (1965)

Solomon Islands (1978)

South Africa (1931; left 1961; rejoined 1994)

Sri Lanka (1948)

Swaziland (1968)

Tanzania (1961)

Tonga (1970)

Trinidad & Tobago (1962)

Tuvalu (1978)

Uganda (1962)

United Kingdom

Vanuatu (1980)

Western Samoa (1970)

Zambia (1964)

Zimbabwe (1980)

Countries which have left the Commonwealth:
Republic of Ireland (1949); Fiji (1987).
*Suspended in 1995.

European Union

Founded in 1957 as the European Economic Community to establish a Common Market.

Later became the EC (European Community) and in 1993 the EU (European Union).

Members (and date of joining; founder members in italics)

Austria (1995)*

Belgium (1958)*

Denmark (1973)

Finland (1995)*

France (1958)*

Germany (1958)*

Greece (1981)

Ireland, Rep. of (1973)*

Italy (1958)*

Luxembourg (1958)*

Netherlands (1958)*

Portugal (1986)*

Spain (1986)*

Sweden (1995)

United Kingdom (1973)

*Founder members of the European single currency (1999).

ECOWAS (Economic Community of West African States)

Founded in 1975 for the promotion of economic cooperation and development by the Treaty of Lagos.

Members

Benin

Burkino Faso

Cape Verde

Gambia

Ghana

Guinea

Guinea-Bissau

Liberia

Mali

Mauritania

Niger

Nigeria

Senegal

Sierra Leone

Togo

EFTA (European Free Trade Association)

Established in 1960.

Members*

Iceland Liechtenstein   Norway Switzerland

Founding members Austria, Denmark, Finland, Portugal, Sweden and UK left to join the EU.

ESA (European Space Agency)

Founded in 1975. Engages its members in space research and technology.

Members

Austria	Germany	Spain
Belgium	Ireland, Rep. of	Sweden
Denmark	Italy	Switzerland
Finland	Netherlands	United Kingdom
France	Norway	

Canada is a cooperating state.

NATO (North Atlantic Treaty Organization)

Founded in 1949.

Original members

Belgium	Iceland	Norway
Canada	Italy	Portugal
Denmark	Luxembourg	United Kingdom
France	Netherlands	United States

Greece and Turkey were both admitted in 1952, the Federal Republic of Germany was admitted in 1955 (and reunited Germany in 1990); Spain joined in 1982.

OAS (Organization of American States)

Founded in 1948 to promote peace, security and the economic development of the western hemisphere.

Original members

Antigua & Barbuda	Guyana
Argentina	Haiti
Bahamas	Honduras
Barbados	Jamaica
Belize	Mexico
Bolivia	Nicaragua
Brazil	Panama
Canada	Paraguay
Chile	Peru
Colombia	St Christopher & Nevis
Costa Rica	St Lucia
Cuba (suspended 1962)	St Vincent & the Grenadines
Dominica	Suriname
Dominican Republic	Trinidad & Tobago
Ecuador	United States of America
El Salvador	Uruguay
Grenada	Venezuela
Guatemala	Guatemala

EU and 39 non-American states have permanent observer status.

OAU (Organization of African Unity)

Established in 1963 to eradicate colonialism and improve economic, cultural and political cooperation in Africa.

Members

Algeria	Eritrea	Nigeria
Angola	Ethiopia	Rwanda
Benin	Gabon	São Tomé &
Botswana	Gambia	Principe
Burkina Faso	Ghana	Senegal
Burundi	Guinea	Seychelles
Cameroon	Guinea-Bissau	Sierra Leone
Cape Verde	Kenya	Somalia
Central African	Lesotho	South Africa
Republic	Liberia	Sudan
Chad	Libya	Swaziland
Comoros	Madagascar	Tanzania
Congo, Rep. of	Malawi	Togo
Congo, Dem.	Mali	Tunisia
Rep. of	Mauritania	Uganda
Côte d'Ivoire	Mauritius	Zambia
Djibouti	Mozambique	Zimbabwe
Egypt	Namibia	
Equatorial Guinea	Niger	

OECD (Organization for Economic Cooperation and Development)

Founded in 1961 to promote the economic growth of the member countries, to coordinate and improve development aid and to expand world trade.

Members

Australia	Hungary	Norway
Austria	Iceland	Poland
Belgium	Ireland, Rep. of	Portugal
Canada	Italy	Spain
Czech Republic	Japan	Sweden
Denmark	Korea, Rep. of	Switzerland
Finland	Luxembourg	Turkey
France	Mexico	United Kingdom
Germany	Netherlands	United States of
Greece	New Zealand	America

OPEC (Organization of the Petroleum Exporting Countries)

Established in 1960 to coordinate price and supply policies of oil-producing states.

Members*

Algeria	Kuwait	Saudi Arabia
Indonesia	Libya	United Arab
Iran	Nigeria	Emirates
Iraq	Qatar	Venezuela

Ecuador withdrew in 1992 and Gabon in 1995.

United Nations

Founded in 1945.

The six main organs are:

General Assembly	Assembly of all members.
Security Council	15 members – 5 permanent (China, France, Russia, UK, US), 10 non-permanent members elected for a 2-year period.
Economic and Social Council	54 non-permanent members elected for a 3-year period.
Trusteeship Council	China, France, Russia, UK, US.
International Court of Justice	Main judicial organ of the UN. Consists of 15 judges, each from a different member state chosen by the General Assembly and the Security Council for a 9-year term. Sits at The Hague.
Secretariat	Secretary-General and a large international staff. Secretary-General is the chief administration officer and serves a 5-year term.

Specialized agencies of the UN and their affiliation dates:

FAO	Food and Agriculture Organization (1945)
IAEA	International Atomic Energy Agency (1957)
IBRD	International Bank for Reconstruction and Development (1945)
ICAO	International Civil Aviation Organization (1947)

Specialized agencies *cont.*

IDA	International Development Association (1960)
IFC	International Finance Corporation (1956)
IFAD	International Fund for Agricultural Development (1977)
ILO	International Labour Organization (1946)
IMO	International Maritime Organization (1948)
IMF	International Monetary Fund (1945)
ITU	International Telecommunications Union (1947)
UNESCO	United Nations Education Scientific and Cultural Organization (1946)
UPU	Universal Postal Union (1947)
WHO	World Health Organization (1948)
WIPO	World Intellectual Property Organization (1974)
WMO	World Meteorological Organization (1950)
WTO	World Trade Organization (1995)

Other agencies

UNHCR	UN High Commission for Refugees
UNICEF	UN International Children's Emergency Fund
UNIDO	UN Industrial Development Organization
UNRRA	UN Relief and Rehabilitation Administration
IUCN	International Union for the Conservation of Nature and Natural Resources

Members (and date of joining)

Afghanistan	1946	Burundi	1962
Albania	1955	Cambodia	1955
Algeria	1962	Cameroon	1960
Andorra	1993	*Canada*	1945
Angola	1976	Cape Verde	1975
Antigua & Barbuda	1981	Central African Rep.	1960
Argentina	1945	Chad	1960
Armenia	1992	*Chile*	1945
Australia	1945	*China**	1945
Austria	1955	*Colombia*	1945
Azerbaijan	1992	Comoros	1975
Bahamas	1973	Congo, Rep. of	1960
Bahrain	1971	Congo, Dem. Rep. of **	1960
Bangladesh	1974	*Costa Rica*	1945
Barbados	1966	Côte d'Ivoire	1960
Belarus	1945	Croatia	1992
Belgium	1945	*Cuba*	1945
Belize	1981	Cyprus	1960
Benin	1960	*Czechoslovakia*	1945–93
Bhutan	1971	Czech Republic	1993
Bolivia	1945	*Denmark*	1945
Bosnia-Herzegovina	1992	Djibouti	1977
Botswana	1966	Dominica	1978
Brazil	1945	*Dominican Republic*	1945
Brunei	1984	*Ecuador*	1945
Bulgaria	1955	*Egypt*	1945
Burkina Faso	1960	*El Salvador*	1945

* *Taiwan to 1971* ** *Formerly Zaire*

Members (and date of joining) *cont.*

Equatorial Guinea	1968	Italy	1955
Eritrea	1993	Jamaica	1962
Estonia	1991	Japan	1956
Ethiopia	1945	Jordan	1955
Fed. States of Micronesia	1991	Kazakstan	1992
Fiji	1970	Kenya	1963
Finland	1955	Korea, Dem. People's	
France	1945	Rep. (N)	1991
Gabon	1960	Korea, Rep. of (S)	1991
Gambia, The	1965	Kuwait	1963
Georgia	1992	Kyrgyzstan	1992
Germany	1973	Laos	1955
Ghana	1957	Latvia	1991
Greece	1945	*Lebanon*	1945
Grenada	1974	Lesotho	1966
Guatemala	1945	*Liberia*	1945
Guinea	1958	Libya	1955
Guinea-Bissau	1974	Liechtenstein	1990
Guyana	1966	Lithuania	1991
Haiti	1945	*Luxembourg*	1945
Honduras	1945	Macedonia	1993
Hungary	1955	Madagascar	1960
Iceland	1946	Malawi	1964
India	1945	Malaysia	1957
Indonesia	1950	Maldives	1965
Iran	1945	Mali	1960
Iraq	1945	Malta	1964
Ireland, Rep. of	1955	Marshall Islands	1991
Israel	1949	Mauritania	1961

Members (and date of joining) *cont.*

Mauritius	1968	Rwanda	1962
Mexico	1945	St Christopher & Nevis	1983
Moldova	1992	St Lucia	1979
Monaco	1991	St Vincent & the	
Mongolia	1961	Grenadines	1980
Morocco	1956	San Marino	1992
Mozambique	1975	São Tomé & Principe	1975
Myanmar (Burma)	1948	*Saudi Arabia*	1945
Namibia	1990	Senegal	1960
Nepal	1955	Seychelles	1976
Netherlands	1945	Sierra Leone	1961
New Zealand	1945	Singapore	1965
Nicaragua	1945	Slovakia	1993
Niger	1960	Slovenia	1991
Nigeria	1960	Solomon Islands	1978
Norway	1945	Somalia	1960
Oman	1971	*South Africa*	1945
Pakistan	1947	Spain	1955
Palau	1994	Sri Lanka	1955
Panama	1945	Sudan	1956
Papua New Guinea	1975	Suriname	1975
Paraguay	1945	Swaziland	1968
Peru	1945	Sweden	1946
Philippines	1945	*Syria*	1945
Poland	1945	Tajikistan	1992
Portugal	1955	Tanzania	1961
Qatar	1971	Thailand	1946
Romania	1955	Togo	1960
Russia	1991	Trinidad & Tobago	1962

Members (and date of joining) *cont.*

Tunisia	1956	Vanuatu	1981
Turkey	1945	*Venezuela*	1945
Turkmenistan	1992	Vietnam	1977
Uganda	1962	Western Samoa	1976
Ukraine	1945	Yemen Arab Rep. (N)	1947–90
United Arab Emirates	1971	Yemen PDR (S)	1967–90
United Kingdom	1945	Yemen	1990
United States of America	1945	*Yugoslavia*	1945–92*
Uruguay	1945	Zambia	1964
USSR	1945–91	Zimbabwe	1980
Uzbekistan	1992		

* Yugoslavia was suspended in 1992
Note: Founder members are in italic type.

ADMINISTRATION AREAS

Pre-1974 Counties of the United Kingdom

England

County	Abbreviation	County Town
Bedfordshire	Beds	Bedford
Berkshire	Berks	Reading
Buckinghamshire	Bucks	Aylesbury
Cambridgeshire	Cambs	Cambridge
Cheshire	Ches	Chester
Cornwall	Corn	Bodmin
Cumberland	Cumb	Carlisle
Derbyshire	Derby	Derby
Devon		Exeter

England *cont.*

County	Abbreviation	County Town
Dorset		Dorchester
Durham	Dur	Durham
Essex		Chelmsford
Gloucestershire	Glos	Gloucester
Hampshire	Hants	Winchester
Herefordshire		Hereford
Hertfordshire	Herts	Hertford
Huntingdonshire	Hunts	Huntingdon
Kent		Maidstone
Lancashire	Lancs	Lancaster
Leicestershire	Leics	Leicester
Lincolnshire	Lincs	Lincoln
Middlesex	Middx	Brentford
Norfolk		Norwich
Northamptonshire	Northants	Northampton
Northumberland	Northumb	Newcastle upon Tyne
Nottinghamshire	Notts	Nottingham
Oxfordshire	Oxon	Oxford
Rutland		Oakham
Shropshire	Salop	Shrewsbury
Somerset	Som	Taunton
Staffordshire	Staffs	Stafford
Suffolk		Ipswich
Surrey		Kingston upon Thames
Sussex		Lewes
Warwickshire	War	Warwick
Westmorland		Appleby

England *cont.*

County	Abbreviation	County Town
Wiltshire	Wilts	Salisbury
Worcestershire	Worcs	Worcester
Yorkshire	Yorks	York

Scotland

County	County Town
Aberdeenshire	Aberdeen
Angus	Forfar
Argyllshire & Islands	Inveraray
Ayrshire	Ayr
Banffshire	Banff
Berwickshire	Duns
Buteshire & Isle of Arran	Rothesay
Caithness	Wick
Clackmannanshire	Alloa
Dunbartonshire	Dumbarton
Dumfriesshire	Dumfries
East Lothian	Haddington
Fife	Cupar
Inverness-shire	Kinross
Kirkcudbrightshire	Kirkcudbright
Lanarkshire	Lanark
Midlothian	Edinburgh
Morayshire	Elgin
Nairnshire	Nairn
Orkney Islands	Kirkwall
Peeblesshire	Peebles
Perthshire	Perth

Scotland *cont.*

County	County Town
Renfrewshire	Renfrew
Ross & Cromarty and Isle of Lewis	Dingwall
Roxburghshire	Jedburgh
Selkirkshire	Selkirk
Shetland Islands	Lerwick
Stirlingshire	Stirling
Sutherland	Dornoch
West Lothian	Linlithgow
Wigtownshire	Wigtown

Wales

County	County Town
Anglesey	Beaumaris
Brecknockshire	Brecon
Caernarvonshire	Caernarvon
Cardiganshire	Cardigan
Carmarthenshire	Carmarthen
Denbighshire	Ruthin
Flintshire	Mold
Glamorgan	Cardiff
Merionethshire	Dolgelley
Monmouthshire	Monmouth
Montgomeryshire	Welshpool
Pembrokeshire	Haverfordwest
Radnorshire	Presteigne

Northern Ireland

County	County Town
Antrim	Belfast
Armagh	Armagh
Down	Downpatrick
Fermanagh	Enniskillen
Londonderry	Londonderry
Tyrone	Omagh

Post-1974 and post-1996 Counties/Councils/Regions of the United Kingdom

England (1974-96) County

Avon	Greater London
Bedfordshire	Greater Manchester
Berkshire	Hampshire
Buckinghamshire	Hereford & Worcester
Cambridgeshire	Hertfordshire
Cheshire	Humberside
Cleveland	Isle of Wight
Cornwall/Isles of Scilly	Kent
Cumbria	Lancashire
Derbyshire	Leicestershire
Devon	Lincolnshire
Dorset	Merseyside
Durham	Norfolk
East Sussex	Northamptonshire
Essex	Northumberland
Gloucestershire	North Yorkshire

England (1974-96) County *cont.*

Nottinghamshire
Oxfordshire
Shropshire
Somerset
South Yorkshire
Staffordshire
Suffolk

Surrey
Tyne & Wear
Warwickshire
West Midlands
West Sussex
West Yorkshire
Wiltshire

England (post-1996) County Councils

Bedfordshire
Berkshire
Buckinghamshire
Cambridgeshire
Cheshire
Cornwall
Cumbria
Derbyshire
Devon
Dorset
Durham
East Sussex
Essex
Gloucestershire
Hampshire
Hereford & Worcester
Hertfordshire
Isle of Wight
Kent

Lancashire
Leicestershire
Lincolnshire
Norfolk
Northamptonshire
Northumberland
North Yorkshire
Nottinghamshire
Oxfordshire
Shropshire
Somerset
Staffordshire
Suffolk
Surrey
Warwickshire
West Sussex
Wiltshire

Unitary Councils (City status)

Birmingham	Newcastle upon Tyne
Bradford	Portsmouth
Bristol	Salford
Coventry	Sheffield
Derby	Southampton
Kingston upon Hull	Stoke-on-Trent
Leeds	Sunderland
Leicester	Wakefield
Liverpool	York
Manchester	

Note: Since abolition of the Greater London Council in 1986, the government of London has been divided among 32 borough councils and the Corporation of the City of London

Scotland

Region (1975–96)	New Council(s) (post-1996)
Borders	Borders
Central	Clackmannan, Falkirk, Stirling
Dumfries & Galloway	Dumfries & Galloway
Fife	Fife
Grampian	City of Aberdeen, Aberdeenshire, Moray
Highland	Highland
Lothian	East Lothian, City of Edinburgh, Midlothian, West Lothian
Tayside	Angus, City of Dundee, Perth & Kinross

Scotland *cont.*

Region (1975–96)	**New Council(s) (post-1996)**
Strathclyde	Argyll & Bute, East Ayrshire, North Ayrshire, South Ayrshire, West Dunbartonshire, East Dunbartonshire, City of Glasgow, Inverclyde, North Lanarkshire, South Lanarkshire, East Renfrewshire, Renfrewshire
Orkney Islands	Orkney Islands
Shetland Islands	Shetland Islands
Western Isles	Western Isles

Wales Counties (1974-96)

Clwyd	Mid Glamorgan
Dyfed	Powys
Gwent	South Glamorgan
Gwynedd	West Glamorgan

Councils (post 1996)

Anglesey	Denbighshire	Powys
Blaenau Gwent*	Flintshire	Rhondda, Cynon, Taff*
Bridgend*	Gwynedd	
Caerphilly*	Merthyr Tydfil*	Swansea**
Cardiff**	Monmouthshire	Torfaen*
Carmarthenshire	Neath and Port Talbot*	Vale of Glamorgan*
Ceredigion	Newport*	Wrexham*
Conwy*	Pembrokeshire	

*Borough status **City status*

Northern Ireland Districts & Borough Councils* (post-1996)

Antrim*	Coleraine*	Lisburn*
Ards*	Cookstown	Magherafelt
Armagh**	Craigavon*	Moyle
Ballymena*	Derry**	Newtownabbey*
Ballymoney*	Down	Newry & Mourne
Banbridge	Dungannon	North Down*
Belfast**	Fermanagh	Omagh
Carrickfergus	Larne*	Strabane
Castlereagh	Limavady*	

*Borough status **City status

Republic of Ireland Provinces/Counties

Province	County	County Town
Connacht	Galway	Galway
	Leitrim	Carrick-on-Shannon
	Mayo	Castlebar
	Roscommon	Roscommon
	Sligo	Sligo
Leinster	Carlow	Carlow
	Dublin	Dublin
	Kildare	Naas
	Kilkenny	Kilkenny
	Laoighis	Portlaoise
	Longford	Longford
	Louth	Dundalk
	Meath	Trim
	Offaly	Tullamore
	Westmeath	Mullingar

Republic of Ireland Provinces/Counties *cont.*

Province	County	County Town
	Wexford	Wexford
	Wicklow	Wicklow
Munster	Clare	Ennis
	Cork	Cork
	Kerry	Tralee
	Limerick	Limerick
	Tipperary	Clonmel
	Waterford	Waterford
Ulster	Cavan	Cavan
	Donegal	Lifford
	Monaghan	Monaghan

Australian States/Territories and their Capitals

Australian Capital Territory	Canberra
New South Wales	Sydney
Northern Territory	Darwin
Queensland	Brisbane
South Australia	Adelaide
Tasmania	Hobart
Victoria	Melbourne
Western Australia	Perth

Canadian Provinces/Territories and their Capitals

Alberta	Edmonton
British Columbia	Victoria
Manitoba	Winnipeg
New Brunswick	Fredericton
Newfoundland	St John's
Northwest Territories	Yellowknife
Nova Scotia	Halifax
Ontario	Toronto
Prince Edward Island	Charlottetown
Quebec	Quebec
Saskatchewan	Regina
Yukon Territory	Whitehorse

New Zealand Regional and City Councils

Regional Councils

Auckland	Otago
Bay of Plenty	Southland
Canterbury	Taranaki
Hawke's Bay	Waikato
Manawatu-wanganui	Wellington
Northland	West Coast

City Councils

Auckland	Nelson
Christchurch	North Shore
Dunedin	Palmerston North
Hamilton	Porirua
Hutt	Upper Hutt
Invercargill	Waitakere
Manukau	Wellington
Napier	

South African Provinces and their Capitals

Eastern Cape	Bisho
Free State	Bloemfontein
Gauteng	Johannesburg/Pretoria
KwaZulu Natal	Pietermaritzburg/Ulundi
Mpumalanga	Nelspruit
Northern Cape	Kimberley
Northern Transvaal	Pietersburg
North-West	Mmabatho
Western Cape	Cape Town

States of the United States of America

State	Capital	Abbrev	Postal Abbrev	Nickname
Alabama	Montgomery	Ala	AL	Yellowhammer State
Alaska	Juneau	Alas	AK	Last Frontier
Arizona	Phoenix	Ariz	AZ	Grand Canyon State
Arkansas	Little Rock	Ark	AR	The Natural State
California	Sacramento	Calif	CA	Golden State
Colorado	Denver	Colo	CO	Centennial State
Connecticut	Hartford	Conn	CT	Constitution State
Delaware	Dover	Del	DE	Diamond State
Florida	Tallahassee	Fla	FL	Sunshine State
Georgia	Atlanta	Ga	GA	Peach State
Hawaii	Honolulu		HI	Aloha State
Idaho	Boise		ID	Gem State
Illinois	Springfield	Ill	IL	Land of Lincoln
Indiana	Indianapolis	Ind	IN	Hoosier State
Iowa	Des Moines	Ia	IA	Hawkeye State
Kansas	Topeka	Kan	KS	Sunflower State
Kentucky	Frankfort	Ky	KY	Bluegrass State
Louisiana	Baton Rouge	La	LA	Pelican State
Maine	Augusta	Me	ME	Pine Tree State
Maryland	Annapolis	Md	MD	Old Line State
Massachusetts	Boston	Mass	MA	Bay State
Michigan	Lansing	Mich	MI	Great Lakes State
Minnesota	St Paul	Minn	MN	North Star State
Mississippi	Jackson	Miss	MS	Magnolia State
Missouri	Jefferson City	Mo	MO	Show Me State

State	Capital	Abbrev	Postal Abbrev	Nickname
Montana	Helena	Mont	MT	Treasure State
Nebraska	Lincoln	Nebr	NB	Cornhusker State
Nevada	Carson City	Nev	NV	The Silver State
New Hampshire	Concord		NH	Granite State
New Jersey	Trenton		NJ	Garden State
New Mexico	Santa Fe	NMex	NM	Land of Enchantment
New York	Albany		NY	Empire State
North Carolina	Raleigh		NC	Tar Heel State
North Dakota	Bismarck	NDak	ND	Peace Garden State
Ohio	Columbus		OH	Buckeye State
Oklahoma	Oklahoma City	Okla	OK	Sooner State
Oregon	Salem	Oreg	OR	Beaver State
Pennsylvania	Harrisburg	Pa	PA	Keystone State
Rhode Island	Providence		RI	The Ocean State
South Carolina	Columbia		SC	Palmetto State
South Dakota	Pierre	SDak	SD	Mount Rushmore State
Tennessee	Nashville	Tenn	TN	Volunteer State
Texas	Austin	Tex	TX	Lone Star State
Utah	Salt Lake City		UT	Beehive State
Vermont	Montpelier	Vt	VT	Green Mountain State
Virginia	Richmond	Va	VA	The Old Dominion State
Washington	Olympia	Wash	WA	Evergreen State
West Virginia	Charleston	WVa	WV	Mountain State
Wisconsin	Madison	Wis	WI	Badger State
Wyoming	Cheyenne	Wyo	WY	Equality State/Cowboy State

History

SOVEREIGNS OF THE BRITISH ISLES

Rulers of Scotland (from 1058)

House of Dunkeld

Malcolm III (Canmore)	1058–93
Donald Ban	1093–4
Duncan II	1094
Donald Ban (*restored*)	1094–7
Edgar	1097–07
Alexander I (the Fierce)	1107–24
David I (the Saint)	1124–53
Malcolm IV (the Maiden)	1153–65
William I (the Lion)	1165–1214
Alexander II	1214–49
Alexander III	1249–86
Margaret, Maid of Norway	1286–1290
John Balliol	1292–6
Robert I (the Bruce)	1306–29
David II	1329–71

House of Stuart

Robert II	1371–90
Robert III	1390–1406
James I	1406–37
James II	1437–60
James III	1460–88
James IV	1488–1513
James V	1513–42
Mary, Queen of Scots	1542–67
James VI (*ascended the throne of England 1603*)	1567–1625

Principal rulers of Wales (from 999)

Deheubarth (Seisyllwg, Brycheiniog and Dyfed)

Llywelyn ap Seisyll	1018–23
Rhydderch ap Iestyn (usurper)	1023
Maredudd ap Edwin	1033–35
Hywel ap Edwin	1033, 1042–4
Gruffyd ap Llywelyn (King of Gwynedd & Powys from 1039)	
Gruffyd ap Llywelyn (second time)	1055–63
Maredudd ab Owain ab Edwin	c.1064
Rhys ap Owain	1072
Rhys ap Tewdwr	1078
Gruffydd ap Rhys	1135
Anarawd ap Gruffydd	1137–43
Cadell ap Gruffydd	1137–c.1151
Maredudd ap Gruffydd	c.1151–55
Rhys ap Gruffydd	c.1151–97

Gwynedd

Cynan ap Hywel	999
Llywelyn ap Seisyll	1005
Iago ap Idwal ap Meurig	1023–39
Gwynedd & Powys annexed by Gruffydd ap Llywelyn, King of Deheubarth	1039
Bleddyn ap Cynfyn ap Gwerstan	1063
Trahaearn ap Caradog (twice)	1075
Gruffydd ap Cynan ap Iago	1075, 1081, c.1094
Owain Gwynedd	1137–70
Gwynedd divided between Cadwaladr ap Gruffydd and his sons	1170–1200

Morgannwg (Glywysing and Gwent)

Rhys ap Owain ap Morgan	?
Hywel ap Owain ap Morgan	?
Meurig ap Hywel seized Gwent	c.1040
Cadwgan ap Meurig	c.1040–c.1055
Morgannwg taken by Llywelyn ap Iorwerth, King of Gwynedd	1055
Cadwgan ap Meurig (second time)	1063
Caradog ap Gruffydd ap Rhydderch	
Iestyn ap Gwrgant (usurper) dispossessed by King William	c.1073
Rufus of England	1081–c.1093

Powys

Held by Gruffydd ap Llywelyn, of Deheubarth	1039–63
Bleddyn ap Cynfyn ap Gwerstan/Rhiwallon ap Cynfyn (d. 1070)	1063
Madog ap Bleddyn/Rhirid ap Bleddyn	1075–88
Cadwgan ap Bleddyn	1075–1109
Madog ap Rhirid/Ithel ap Rhirid	1109–10
Territory frequently divided	1110–1200

By 1200 Welsh kings were lords owing allegiance to England and by 1282 Edward I had conquered Wales. His son was the first English Prince of Wales (b. Caernarfon, 25 April 1284).

Rulers of Ireland (from 1002)*

Máelsechnaill mac Domnaill	(d. 1022)
Brian Bóruma mac Cennétig	(d. 1014)
Tairrdelbach Ua Briain	(d. 1086)
Muirchertach Ua Briain	(d. 1119)
Domnall Ua Lochlainn	(d. 1121)
Tairrdelbach Ua Conchobair	(d. 1156)
Muirchertach mac Lochlainn	(d. 1166)
Ruaidrí Ua Conchobair	(d. 1198)**

The most powerful kings of the pre-Norman period.
* *The last native King of Ireland. The Pope granted Ireland to King Henry II of England in 1172. Viking power in Ireland ended at the Battle of Clontarf in 1014. The 150 years of fighting which followed for the High Kingship contributed largely to the end of Irish royal rule.*

Rulers of England (from 955) and of the United Kingdom (from 1801)

Saxon Line

Edwy	955–9
Edgar	959–75
Edward the Martyr	975–8
Ethelred the Unready	978–1016
Edmund Ironside	1016

Danish Line

Canute (Cnut)	1016–35
Harold I	1035–40
Hardicanute (Harthacnut)	1040–2

Saxon Line

Edward the Confessor	1042–66
Harold II (Godwinson)	1066

House of Normandy

William I (The Conqueror)	1066–87
William II	1087–1100
Henry I	1100–35
Stephen	1135–54

House of Plantagenet

Henry II (Curtmantel)	1154–89
Richard (The Lionheart)	1189–99
John (Lackland)	1199–1216
Henry III	1216–72
Edward I (Hammer of the Scots)	1272–1307
Edward II	1307–27
Edward III	1327–77
Richard II	1377–99

House of Lancaster

Henry IV	1399–1413
Henry V	1413–22
Henry VI	1422–61

House of York

Edward IV	1461–83
Edward V	1483
Richard III (Crookback)	1483–5

House of Tudor

Henry VII	1485–1509
Henry VIII	1509–47
Edward VI	1547–53
Jane (The Nine Days' Queen)	1553
Mary I (Bloody Mary)	1553–8
Elizabeth I (The Virgin Queen)	1558–1603

House of Stuart

James I of England and VI of Scotland	1603–25
Charles I	1625–49

Commonwealth (declared 1649)

Oliver Cromwell, Lord Protector	1653–8
Richard Cromwell	1658–9

House of Stuart

Charles II	1660–85
James II of England and VII of Scotland	1685–8
William III and Mary II (Mary d. 1694)	1689–1702
Anne	1702–14

House of Hanover

George I	1714–27
George II	1727–60
George III (Farmer George)	1760–1820
George IV	1820–30
William IV (Silly Billy)	1830–7
Victoria	1837–1901

House of Saxe-Coburg-Gotha

Edward VII	1901–10

House of Windsor*

George V (The Sailor King)	1910–36
Edward VIII (Our Smiling Prince)	1936
George VI	1936–52
Elizabeth II	1952–

George V, originally of the House of Saxe-Coburg-Gotha, decreed on 17 July 1917 that in future it would be known as the House of Windsor, because of anti-German feeling in the First World War.

BRITISH PRIME MINISTERS

Monarch	Prime Minister	Party	Term of Office
George II	Sir Robert Walpole	Whig	1721–42
	Earl of Wilmington	Whig	1742–3
	Henry Pelham	Whig	1743–54
	Duke of Newcastle	Whig	1754–6
	Duke of Devonshire	Whig	1756–7
	Duke of Newcastle	Whig	1757–60
George III	Duke of Newcastle	Whig	1760–2
	Earl of Bute	Tory	1762–3
	George Grenville	Whig	1763–5
	Marquis of Rockingham	Whig	1766
	Earl of Chatham	Tory	1766–8
	Duke of Grafton	Whig	1768–9
	Lord North	Tory	1770–82
	Marquis of Rockingham	Whig	1782
	Earl of Shelburne	Whig	1782–3

Monarch	Prime Minister	Party	Term of Office
	Duke of Portland	Coalition	1783
	William Pitt	Tory	1783–1801
	Viscount Sidmouth	Tory	1801–4
	William Pitt	Tory	1804–6
	Lord Grenville	Whig	1806–7
	Duke of Portland	Tory	1807–9
	Spencer Perceval	Tory	1809–12
George IV	Earl of Liverpool	Tory	1812–27
	George Canning	Tory	1827
	Viscount Goderich	Tory	1827
	Duke of Wellington	Tory	1827–30
William IV	Earl Grey	Whig	1830–4
	Viscount Melbourne	Whig	1834
	Sir Robert Peel	Tory	1834–5
	Viscount Melbourne	Whig	1835–7
Victoria	Viscount Melbourne	Whig	1837–41
	Sir Robert Peel	Tory	1841–6
	Lord John Russell	Whig	1846–52
	Earl of Derby	Tory	1852
	Earl of Aberdeen	Peelite	1852–5
	Viscount Palmerston	Liberal	1855–8
	Earl of Derby	Tory	1858–9
	Viscount Palmerston	Liberal	1859–65
	Lord John Russell	Liberal	1865–6
	Earl of Derby	Conservative	1866–8
	Benjamin Disraeli	Conservative	1868
	W E Gladstone	Liberal	1868–74
	Benjamin Disraeli	Conservative	1874–80
	W E Gladstone	Liberal	1880–5
	Marquis of Salisbury	Conservative	1885–6
	W E Gladstone	Liberal	1886
	Marquis of Salisbury	Conservative	1886–92

Monarch	Prime Minister	Party	Term of Office
	W E Gladstone	Liberal	1892–4
	Earl of Rosebery	Liberal	1894–5
	Marquis of Salisbury	Conservative	1895–1901
Edward VII	Marquis of Salisbury	Conservative	1901–2
	A J Balfour	Conservative	1902–5
	Sir H Campbell-Bannerman	LIberal	1905–8
	H H Asquith	Liberal	1908–10
George V	H H Asquith	Liberal	1910–15
	H H Asquith	Coalition	1915–16
	D Lloyd George	Coalition	1916–22
	A Bonar Law	Conservative	1922–3
	S Baldwin	Conservative	1923–4
	J R Macdonald	Labour	1924
	S Baldwin	Conservative	1924–9
	J R Macdonald	Labour	1929–31
	J R Macdonald	National	1931–5
	S Baldwin	National	1935–6
Edward VIII (abdicated 1936)			
George VI	S Baldwin	National	1936–7
	A N Chamberlain	National	1937–9
	A N Chamberlain	War Cabinet	1939–40
	W S Churchill	War Cabinet	1940–5
	W S Churchill	Caretaker	1945
	C R Attlee	Labour	1945–51
	Sir W S Churchill	Conservative	1951–2
Elizabeth II	Sir W S Churchill	Conservative	1952–5
	Sir A Eden	Conservative	1955–7
	H Macmillan	Conservative	1957–63
	Sir A Douglas-Home	Conservative	1963–4
	H Wilson	Labour	1964–70

Monarch	Prime Minister	Party	Term of Office
	E Heath	Conservative	1970–4
	H Wilson	Labour	1974–6
	J Callaghan	Labour	1976–9
	M Thatcher	Conservative	1979–90
	J Major	Conservative	1990–7
	T Blair	Labour	1997–

US PRESIDENTS

President	Party	Term of Office
George Washington	Fed	1789–97
John Adams	Fed	1797–1801
Thomas Jefferson	Rep	1801–9
James Madison	Rep	1809–17
James Monroe	Rep	1817–25
John Quincy Adams	Rep	1825–9
Andrew Jackson	Dem	1829–37
Martin van Buren	Dem	1837–41
William H Harrison	Whig	1841
John Tyler	Whig	1841–5
James K Polk	Dem	1845–9
Zachary Taylor	Whig	1849–50
Millard Fillmore	Whig	1850–3
Franklin Pierce	Dem	1853–7
James Buchanan	Dem	1857–61
Abraham Lincoln	Rep	1861–5
Andrew Johnson	Rep	1865–9

President	Party	Term of Office
Ulysses S Grant	Rep	1869–77
Rutherford B Hayes	Rep	1877–81
James A Garfield	Rep	1881
Chester A Arthur	Rep	1881–5
Grover Cleveland	Dem	1885–9
Benjamin Harrison	Rep	1889–93
Grover Cleveland	Dem	1893–7
William McKinley	Rep	1897–1901
Theodore Roosevelt	Rep	1901–9
William Howard Taft	Rep	1909–13
Woodrow Wilson	Dem	1913–21
Warren G Harding	Rep	1921–3
Calvin Coolidge	Rep	1923–9
Herbert C Hoover	Rep	1929–33
Franklin D Roosevelt	Dem	1933–45
Harry S Truman	Dem	1945–53
Dwight D Eisenhower	Rep	1953–61
John F Kennedy	Dem	1961–3
Lyndon B Johnson	Dem	1963–9
Richard M Nixon	Rep	1969–74
Gerald R Ford	Rep	1974–7
James Carter	Dem	1977–81
Ronald Reagan	Rep	1981–9
George Bush	Rep	1989–93
William Jefferson Clinton	Dem	1993–2001
George W. Bush	Rep	2001–

AUSTRALIAN PRIME MINISTERS

Name	Appointed
Edmund Barton	1901
Alfred Deakin	1903; 1905; 1909
J C Watson	1904
George Reid	1904
Andrew Fisher	1908; 1914
Joseph Cook	1913
W Hughes	1915
S M Bruce	1923
J H Scullin	1929
J A Lyons	1932
Sir Earle Page	1939
R W G Menzies	1939; 1949
A W Fadden	1941
John Curtin	1941
F M Forde	1945
J B Chifley	1945
Harold Edward Holt	1966
John G Gorton	1968
William McMahon	1971
E G Whitlam	1972
Malcolm Fraser	1975
R J L Hawke	1983
Paul Keating	1991
John Howard	1996

NEW ZEALAND PRIME MINISTERS

Name	Appointed
William Hall-Jones	1906
Sir Joseph George Ward	1906; 1928
Thomas MacKenzie	1912
William Ferguson Massey	1912; 1919
Sir Francis Henry Dillon Bell	1925
Joseph Gordon Coates	1925
George William Forbes	1930; 1931
Michael Joseph Savage	1935
Peter Fraser	1940
Sidney George Holland	1949
Sir Keith Jacka Holyoake	1957; 1960
Walter Nash	1957
John Ross Marshall (later Sir)	1972
Norman Eric Kirk	1973
Wallace Edward Rowling	1974
Sir Robert David Muldoon	1975
David Russell Lange	1984
Geoffrey Winston Russell Palmer	1989
J B Bolger	1990
Jenny Shipley	1997
Helen Clark	1999

CANADIAN PRIME MINISTERS

Name	Appointed
John Alexander MacDonald	1867;1878
Alexander Mackenzie	1873
John J C Abbot	1891
John S D Thompson	1892
Mackenzie Bowell	1894
Charles Tupper	1896
Wilfrid Laurier	1896
Robert Laird Borden	1911
Arthur Meighen	1920;1926
William Lyon Mackenzie King	1921;1926;1935
Richard Bedford Bennett	1930
Louis Stephen St Laurent	1948
John George Diefenbaker	1957
Lester Bowles Pearson	1963
Pierre Elliot Trudeau	1968;1980
Joseph Clark	1979
John Napier Turner	1984
M Brian Mulroney	1984
Kim Campbell	1993
Jean Chrétien	1993

Geography

BEAUFORT SCALE

Scale No.	Description	Speed mph (kph)	Characteristics on land
0	Calm	Less than 1 (1)	Smoke goes straight up
1	Light air	1-3 (1-5)	Smoke blows in wind
2	Light breeze	4-7 (6-12)	Wind felt on face; leaves rustle
3	Gentle breeze	8-12 (13-20)	Light flag flutters; leaves in constant motion
4	Moderate breeze	13-18 (21-29)	Dust and loose paper blown. Small branches move
5	Fresh breeze	19-24 (30-39)	Small trees sway
6	Strong breeze	25-31 (40-50)	Hard to use umbrellas. Whistling heard in telegraph wires
7	Moderate gale	32-38 (51-61)	Hard to walk into. Whole trees in motion
8	Fresh gale	39-46 (62-74)	Twigs break off trees
9	Strong gale	47-54 (75-87)	Chimney pots and slates lost
10	Whole gale	55-63 (88-102)	Trees uprooted. Considerable structural damage
11	Storm	64-75 (103-120)	Widespread damage
12-17	Hurricane	over 75 (120)	Violent, massive damage

The measurement of wind speed.

Characteristics at sea

Sea like a mirror

Ripples formed, but without foam crests

Small wavelets. Crests glassy but do not break

Large wavelets. Crests begin to break. Foam glassy, scattered white horses

Small waves. Fairly frequent white horses

Moderate waves. Many white horses. Chance of spray

Large waves, extensive white foam crests. Probably spray

Sea leaps up. White foam from breaking waves begins to be blown in streaks along wind direction

Moderately high waves. Edges of crests begin to break into the spindrift. Foam blown in well-marked streaks along wind direction

High waves. Dense streaks of foam along wind direction. Crests topple, tumble and roll over. Spray may affect visibility

Very high waves with long overhanging crests. Foam is blown in great patches along wind direction. Surface takes on a general white appearance. Visibility affected

Exceptionally high waves. Sea completely covered with long white patches of foam lying along wind direction. Visibility affected

Air is filled with foam and spray. Sea completely white with driving spray. Visibility seriously affected

RICHTER AND MERCALLI SCALES

The magnitude of earthquakes is measured in units on the Richter Scale and their intensity on the Mercalli Scale.

Mercalli	Richter	Characteristics
1	less than 3.5	Only detected by seismograph
2	3.5	Only noticed by people at rest
3	4.2	Similar to vibrations from HGV
4	4.5	Felt indoors; rocks parked cars
5	4.8	Generally felt; awakens sleepers
6	5.4	Trees sway; causes some damage
7	6.1	Causes general alarm; building walls crack
8	6.5	Walls collapse
9	6.9	Some houses collapse; cracks appear in ground
10	7.3	Buildings destroyed; rails buckle
11	8.1	Most buildings destroyed; landslides
12	greater than 8.1	Total destruction of area

SHIPPING AREAS

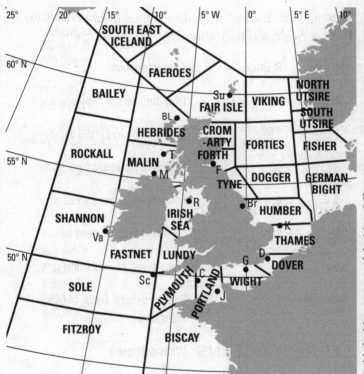

Published by courtesy of the Met. Office.

T	Tiree	**G**	Greenwich light vessel
BL	Butt of Lewis		automatic ('Greenwich LV auto')
Su	Sumburgh	**C**	Channel
F	Fifeness	**Sc**	Scilly auto
Br	Bridlington	**Va**	Valentia
D	Dover	**R**	Ronaldsway
J	Jersey	**M**	Malin Head

CONTINENTS OF THE WORLD

Name	Area (sq km)
Asia	43,998,000
America*	41,918,000
Africa	29,800,000
Antarctica	13,980,000
Europe**	9,699,000
Oceania***	7,618,490

*Usually divided politically into North/Central and South America; North/Central America is approx. 24,255,000 sq km
**Including European Russia
***Australia, New Zealand and non-Asian Pacific islands

LARGEST ISLANDS

Name	Ocean	Area (sq km)
Greenland	Arctic	2,175,600
New Guinea	Pacific	821,030
Borneo	Pacific	744,366
Madagascar	Indian	587,040
Baffin	Arctic	476,068

LARGEST OCEANS

Name	Area (sq km)	Greatest depth (m)
Pacific	165,241,000	11,020
Atlantic	86,550,000	9,460
Indian	73,427,000	7,542
Arctic	13,230,000	5,400

LARGEST SEAS

Name	Area (sq km)	Greatest depth (m)
South China	2,974,600	7,260
Caribbean	2,753,000	8,600
Mediterranean	2,503,000	5,100
Bering	2,226,100	3,930
Gulf of Mexico	1,542,985	3,505

LARGEST DESERTS

Name	Continent	Area (sq km)
Sahara	Africa	8,400,000
Australian	Australia	1,550,000
Arabian	Asia	1,300,000
Gobi	Asia	1,040,000
Kalahari	Africa	520,000

HIGHEST MOUNTAINS

Name (all in Himalayas)	Height (m)
Everest	8,863
K2	8,607
Kangchenjunga	8,597
Lhotse	8,511
Makulu I	8,481

HIGHEST VOLCANOES (ACTIVE)

Name	Country	Height (m)
Gullatiri	Chile	6,060
Cotopaxi	Ecuador	5,897
Tupungatito	Chile	5,640
Lascar	Chile	5,590
Nevado del Ruiz	Colombia	5,400

HIGHEST WATERFALLS

Name	Country	Height (m)
Angel	Venezuela	979
Tugela	South Africa	947
Utigard	Norway	800
Mongefossen	Norway	774
Yosemite	USA	739

LONGEST RIVERS

Name	Continent	Length (km)
Nile	Africa	6,670
Amazon	S America	6,448
Yangtze-Kiang	Asia	6,300
Mississippi-Missouri	N America	6,020
Yenisey-Angara	Asia	5,540

LARGEST LAKES

Name	Continent	Area (sq km)
Caspian Sea	Asia	380,000
Superior	N America	82,100
Victoria	Africa	69,485
Aral Sea*	Asia	64,000
Huron	N America	59,600

*Saltwater

DEEPEST CAVES

Name	Country	Depth (m)
Reseau Jean Bernard	France	1,602
Shakta Pantjukhina	Georgia	1,508
Sistema del Trave	Spain	1,441
Aminakoateak	Spain	1,408
Snezhnaya	Georgia	1,370

LARGEST COUNTRIES (AREA)

Name	Area (sq km)
Russian Federation	17,070,289
Canada	9,970,537
China	9,596,961
USA	9,155,579
Brazil	8,511,965

LARGEST COUNTRIES (POPULATION)

Name	Population
China, People's Rep. of	1,232,083,000
India	970,930,000
USA	270,298,524
Indonesia	196,813,000
Brazil	157,872,000

SMALLEST COUNTRIES (AREA)

Name	Area (sq km)
Vatican City State	0.51
Monaco	1.95
Nauru	21.3
Tuvalu	26.0
San Marino	61.0

SMALLEST COUNTRIES (POPULATION)

Name	Population
Vatican City State	1000
Tuvalu	10,000
Nauru	11,000
San Marino	25,000
Liechtenstein	31,000

MOST DENSELY-POPULATED COUNTRIES

Name	People per sq km
Monaco	21,500
Singapore	5,000
Vatican City State	2,270
Bahrein	863
Bangladesh	834

Greenland is the least densely populated country with one person per 37.5 sq km; the UK has 243 people per sq km. Estimates put the world population today at 6 billion, rising to 8.9 billion by 2050.

LARGEST CITIES

Name	Country	Population (millions)
Tokyo/Yokohama	Japan	28.7
Mumbai (Bombay)	India	27.5
Lagos	Nigeria	24.0
Shanghai	China	23.0
Jakarta	Indonesia	21.0

LONGEST ROAD TUNNELS

Name	Country	Length (km)
St Gotthard	Switzerland	16.32
Arlberg	Austria	13.98
Fréjus	France/Italy	12.90
Mont Blanc	France/Italy	11.60
Gudvangen	Norway	11.40

LONGEST BRIDGES (MAIN SPAN)

Name	Country	Length (m)
Akashi Kaikyo	Japan	1990
Store Baelt	Denmark	1624
Humber Estuary	England	1410
Verrazano Narrows	USA	1298
Golden Gate	USA	1280

LONGEST RAIL TUNNELS

Name	Country	Length (km)
Seikan	Japan	53.90
Channel Tunnel	France/Eng	49.94
Moscow Metro, Belyaevo-Medvekov	Russia	30.60
London Underground, E Finchley-Morden	England	27.84
Oshimizu	Japan	22.17

LONGEST SHIP CANALS

Name	Country	Length (km)
St Lawrence Seaway	Canada/USA	304
Main-Danube	Germany	171
Suez	Egypt	162
Albert	Belgium	129
Kiel	Germany	98

HIGHEST DAMS

Name	Country	Height (m)
Rogun	Tajikistan	335
Nurek	Tajikistan	300
Hsaio Wang	China	296
Grande Dixence	Switzerland	285
Inguri	Georgia	272

BUSIEST PORTS

Name	Country	Million tonnes
Rotterdam	Netherlands	350.0
Singapore	Singapore	290.0
Kobe	Japan	171.0
Hong Kong	China	147.2
Shanghai	China	139.6

BUSIEST AIRPORTS (TOTAL PASSENGERS)

City	Name	Country	Passengers (millions)
Chicago	O'Hare Intl.	USA	65.0
Dallas	Dallas/Ft Worth Intl .	USA	51.2
Los Angeles	Los Angeles Intl.	USA	48.1
London	Heathrow	UK	47.6
Atlanta	Hartsfield	USA	47.4

BUSIEST AIRPORTS (INTL. PASSENGERS)

City	Name	Country	Passengers (millions)
London	Heathrow	UK	38.0
Frankfurt	Frankfurt	Germany	23.7
Paris	Charles de Gaulle	France	22.4
Hong Kong	Hong Kong Intl.	China	22.1
Tokyo	New Tokyo Intl.	Japan	19.0

Religion

THE TEN COMMANDMENTS

Exodus 20: 1–17 (from the *Good News Bible*)

God spoke, and these were his words: 2 'I am the Lord your God who brought you out of Egypt, where you were slaves.

3 'Worship no god but me.

4 'Do not make for yourselves images of anything in heaven or on earth or in the water under the earth.

5 Do not bow down to any idol or worship it, because I am the Lord your God and I tolerate no rivals. I bring punishment on those who hate me and on their descendants down to the third and fourth generation.

6 But I show my love to thousands of generations of those who love me and obey my laws.

7 'Do not use my name for evil purposes, for I, the Lord your God, will punish anyone who misuses my name.

8 'Observe the Sabbath and keep it holy.

9 You have six days in which to do your work,

10 But the seventh day is a day of rest dedicated to me. On that day no one is to work – neither you, your children, your slaves, your animals, nor the foreigners who live in your country.

11 In six days I, the Lord, made the earth, the sky, the sea, and everything in them, but on the seventh day I rested. That is why I, the Lord, blessed the Sabbath and made it holy.

Exodus 20: 1–17 *cont.*

¹² 'Respect your father and your mother, so that you may live a long time in the land that I am giving you.

¹³ 'Do not commit murder.

¹⁴ 'Do not commit adultery.

¹⁵ 'Do not steal.

¹⁶ 'Do not accuse anyone falsely.

¹⁷ 'Do not desire another man's house; do not desire his wife, his slaves, his cattle, his donkeys, or anything else that he owns.'

THE BEATITUDES

Matthew 5:3-12 (from the *Good News Bible*)

³ 'Happy are those who know they are spiritually poor; the Kingdom of heaven belongs to them!

⁴ Happy are those who mourn; God will comfort them!

⁵ Happy are those who are humble; they will receive what God has promised!

⁶ Happy are those whose greatest desire is to do what God requires; God will satisfy them fully!

⁷ Happy are those who are merciful to others; God will be merciful to them!

⁸ Happy are the pure in heart; they will see God!

⁹ Happy are those who work for peace; God will call them his children!

Matthew 5:3-12 *cont.*

¹⁰ Happy are those who are persecuted because they do what God requires; the Kingdom of heaven belongs to them!

¹¹ Happy are you when people insult you and persecute you and tell all kinds of evil lies against you because you are my followers.

¹² Be happy and glad, for a great reward is kept for you in heaven. This is how the prophets who lived before you were persecuted.

Scriptures quoted from the Good News Bible *published by the Bible Societies/HarperCollins Publishers Ltd, UK© American Bible Society 1966, 1971, 1976, 1992.*

THE STATIONS OF THE CROSS

A devotional aid to meditation on the Passion of Christ.

1   Jesus is condemned to death.
2   Jesus bears his cross.
3   Jesus falls the first time.
4   Jesus meets his mother.
5   Jesus is helped by Simon.
6   Veronica wipes the face of Jesus.
7   Jesus falls a second time.
8   Jesus consoles the women of Jerusalem.
9   Jesus falls a third time.
10   Jesus is stripped of his garments.
11   Jesus is nailed to the cross.
12   Jesus dies on the cross.
13   Jesus is taken down from the cross.
14   Jesus is laid in the tomb.

THE TWELVE APOSTLES

Andrew	Peter (Simon)
James	John
Philip	Nathanael (Bartholomew)
Matthew (Levi)	Thomas
James (son of Alphaeus)	Judas (brother of James)
Judas Iscariot	Simon the Zealot

After the death of Judas Iscariot, the number was maintained at twelve by the election of Matthias.

THE FOUR LAST THINGS

Death   Judgement   Heaven Hell

THE SEVEN SACRAMENTS

Baptism	Penance	Ordination
Confirmation	Anointing of the	Matrimony
Eucharist	Sick	

THE SEVEN CHAMPIONS OF CHRISTENDOM

Name	Emblem
St George of England	Red cross on white ground
St Andrew of Scotland	Cross saltire gold on blue ground
St David of Wales	Dove
St Patrick of Ireland	Shamrock and snakes
St Denis of France	Carrying his severed head, witness to martyrdom
St James of Spain	Scallop shell
St Antony of Padua (Italy)	Lily, flowered cross and book

THE SEVEN FATHERS OF THE CHURCH

Early bishops and writers on doctrine.

St Athanasius

St Gregory of Nazianzus

St John Chrysostom

St John of Damascus

St Basil of Caesarea

St Gregory of Nyssa

St Cyril of Alexandria

THE TEN PLAGUES OF EGYPT

1 Water turns to blood

2 Frogs

3 Lice, sand flies or fleas

4 Swarms of flies

5 Cattle die from disease

6 Boils and sores

7 Hail

8 Locusts

9 Darkness

10 Death of first-born

THE FOUR HORSEMEN OF THE APOCALYPSE

Revelation 6

Four riders whose arrival symbolizes the end of the world and the devastation and terror accompanying this event.

The rider of the White Horse carries a bow and wears a crown; he represents the Power of God triumphing over evil.

The rider of the fiery Red Horse carries a large sword and represents Bloodshed and War.

The rider of the Black Horse carries a pair of scales and represents Famine.

The rider of the Pale Horse is called Death and is closely followed by Hades; he represents Disease and Death.

THE TWELVE TRIBES OF ISRAEL

Genesis 29–30, 35

The twelve tribes, by tradition, take their roots from the twelve sons of Jacob.

Reuben	Asher
Judah	Joseph
Gad	Levi
Zebulun	Naphtali
Simeon	Issachar
Dan	Benjamin

THE SEVEN LAST PLAGUES

Revelation 16

1 Sores
2 Sea turns to blood
3 Rivers turn to blood
4 People scorched by
   intense heat of sun

5 Darkness
6 River Euphrates dries up
7 Earthquake

THE SEVEN CORPORAL WORKS OF MERCY

Food to the Hungry
Drink to the Thirsty
Clothing to the Naked
Harbouring the Stranger

Visiting the Sick
Ministering to Prisoners
Burying the Dead

SAINTS AND SAINTS' DAYS

The list on pages 93–98 shows a wide cross-section
from the many hundreds of saints who are, or were,
venerated on the days shown. It is not intended to
represent the calendar of any particular denomination.

January

1 Abbot Clarus
2 Basil, Gregory
3 Geneviève
4 Roger of Ellant
5 Simeon Stylites
6 Melanius
7 Raymond of Peñafort
8 Lucian, Nathalan
9 Adrian of Canterbury
10 Peter Orseolo
11 Alexander
12 Benedict Biscop
13 Bishop Hilary
14 Felix of Nola
15 Ita
16 Bernard and his Companions
17 Antony the Abbot
18 Prisca
19 Canute IV, King of Denmark
20 Sebastian, Fabian
21 Agnes
22 Vincent of Saragossa
23 Emerentiana
24 Francis de Sales
25 Dwyn
26 Paula
27 John Chrysostom
28 Thomas Aquinas
29 Gildas
30 Aidan
31 John Bosco

February

1 Brigid of Ireland
2 Joan de Lestonnac
3 Blaise
4 John de Britto, Gilbert of Sempringham
5 Agatha
6 Amand
7 Apollonia
8 Jerome Emiliani
9 Teilo
10 Scholastica
11 Finnian
12 Julian the Hospitaller, Seven Servite Founders
13 Huna
14 Valentine
15 Sigfrid
16 Juliana
17 Finan
18 Colman of Lindisfarne
19 Mesrop
20 Ulric of Haselbury
21 Peter Damian
22 Margaret of Cortona
23 Polycarp
24 Montanus and Lucius
25 Walburga
26 Porphyry of Gaza
27 Gabriel Possenti
28 Oswald

March

1 David
2 Chad
3 Cunegund
4 Adrian of Nicomedia
5 Bishop Ciaran
6 Baldred
7 Perpetua and Felicity
8 John of God
9 Dominic Savio, Frances
   of Rome
10 John Ogilvie
11 Eulogius of Cordoba
12 Pope Gregory the Great
13 Gerald of Mayo
14 Matilda
15 Louise de Marillac
16 Boniface of Ross
17 Joseph of Arimathea, Patrick
18 Fra Angelico, Cyril of
   Jerusalem
19 Joseph
20 Cuthbert
21 Abbot Benedict
22 Zachary
23 Turibius
24 Catherine of Sweden
25 Dismas
26 Ludger
27 Rupert of Salzburg
28 Guntramnus
29 Gwladys
30 John Climacus
31 Benjamin

April

1 Hugh of Grenoble
2 Francis of Paola
3 Richard of Chichester
4 Benedict the Black
5 Vincent Ferrer
6 William of Eskill
7 John Baptist de la Salle
8 Walter of Pontoise
9 Waudru
10 Michael de Sanctis
11 Stanislaus
12 Pope Martin I
13 Guinoch
14 Tiburtius and Valerian
15 Ruadhan
16 Bernadette of Lourdes,
   Magnus of Orkney
17 Donnan
18 Apollonius the Apologist
19 Expeditus
20 Caedwalla, King of Wessex
21 Anselm
22 Theodore of Sykean
23 George
24 Ivo
25 Mark
26 Cletus
27 Zita
28 Peter Mary Chanel
29 Catherine of Siena
30 Adjutor

May

1 Peregrine Laziosi
2 Athanasius
3 Alexander and Eventius
4 Florian
5 Asaph
6 Adbert
7 John of Beverley
8 Victor Maurus
9 Pachomius
10 Cathal
11 Gengulf
12 Pancras
13 Andrew Fournet, Caradoc
14 Apostle Matthias
15 Dympna, Isidore the Farmer
16 Honoratus, John Nepomucen, Ubald
17 Paschal Baylon
18 Venantius, John I
19 Ivo of Kermartin, Pope Celestine V
20 Bernardino of Siena
21 Godric
22 Rita of Cascia
23 William of Rochester
24 David of Scotland
25 Venerable Bede, Gregory VII
26 Philip Neri
27 Augustine of Canterbury
28 Bernard of Montjoux
29 Bona
30 Ferdinand III of Castile
31 Petronilla

June

1 Nicomede
2 Erasmus (Elmo)
3 Charles Lwanga
4 Petroc, Joan of Arc
5 Boniface
6 Norbert
7 Colman of Dromore
8 William of York
9 Columba of Iona
10 Landerious of Paris
11 Barnabas
12 Ternan
13 Antony of Padua
14 Basil the Great
15 Vitus
16 John Francis Regis
17 Alban
18 Mark and Marcellian
19 Romuald
20 Adalbert of Magdeburg, Mary, Our Lady of Consolation
21 Aloysius
22 John Fisher, Thomas More
23 Agrippina
24 John the Baptist
25 Febronia
26 Anthelm
27 Cyril of Alexandria, Kyned
28 Austell
29 Paul, Peter
30 Erentrude

July

1 Oliver Plunkett, Serf
2 Otto
3 Thomas the Apostle
4 Elizabeth of Portugal
5 Modwenna
6 Maria Goretti
7 Hedda of Winchester
8 Bishop Killian
9 Everildis, Virgin Mary, Queen of Peace
10 The Seven Brothers
11 Drostan
12 John Gualbert
13 Henry II
14 Camillus de Lellis
15 Swithin
16 Helier
17 Kenelm
18 Edburga of Winchester
19 Gervase, Protase
20 Margaret (Marina)
21 Laurence of Brindisi
22 Mary Magdalene
23 Apollinaris
24 Gleb, Christina
25 James the Great, Christopher, Margaret
26 Anne
27 The Seven Sleepers of Ephesus
28 Samson
29 Martha
30 Abdon, Sennen
31 Ignatius of Loyola

August

1 Alphonsus Liguori
2 Theodota of Nicaea
3 Germanus of Auxerre
4 John Mary Vianney
5 Afra
6 Justua, Pastor
7 Pope Sixtus II
8 Cyriacus, Dominic
9 Emygdius
10 Lawrence
11 Clare
12 Attracta
13 Hippolytus, Cassian of Imola
14 Athanasia of Aegina
15 Mary the Virgin
16 Roch, Stephen of Hungary
17 Hyacinth
18 Helen
19 John Eudes
20 Bernard of Clairvaux
21 Pope Pius X
22 Symphorian
23 Rose of Lima
24 Bartholomew
25 Louis of France, Genesius the Comedian
26 Ninian
27 Monica
28 Augustine of Hippo
29 Sebbi
30 Felix, Adauctus
31 Raymond Nonnatus, Aidan of Lindisfarne

September

1 Fiacre, Giles
2 Brocard
3 Basilissa
4 Macnissi
5 Lawrence Giustiniani
6 Magnus of Fussen
7 Evurtius
8 Adrian, Natalia
9 Ciaran of Clonmacnoise
10 Nicholas of Tolentino
11 Deiniol
12 Guy of Anderlecht
13 Venerius
14 Notburga
15 Nicomedes
16 Cornelius, Ninian
17 Lambert
18 Joseph of Cupertino
19 Januarius
20 Eustace
21 Matthew
22 Maurice
23 Eunan, Adamnan
24 Gerard of Csanad
25 Finbarr
26 Cosmas and Damian, Cyprian
27 Vincent de Paul
28 Bernard of Feltre
29 Gabriel the Archangel, Michael the Archangel, Raphael the Archangel, Wenceslas
30 Jerome

October

1 Remigius
2 Leger
3 Hewald the Dark and Hewald the Fair
4 Francis of Assisi
5 Maurus, Placid
6 Faith (Foi), Bruno
7 Osith
8 Pelagia the Penitent
9 Denis, Bishop of Paris, John Leonardi
10 Paulinus of York
11 Canice (Kenneth)
12 Ethelburga of Barking
13 Edward the Confessor
14 Callistus I
15 Teresa of Avila
16 Gall, Margaret Mary
17 Ignatius of Antioch, Etheldreda (Audrey)
18 Luke
19 Paul of the Cross
20 Andrew of Crete
21 Fintan Munnu
22 Donatus of Fiesole
23 John Capistrano
24 Antony Claret
25 Crispin and Crispinian, Marnock, Margaret Clitherow
26 Eata
27 Frumentius
28 Simon, Jude
29 Colman of Kilmacduagh
30 Marcellus the Centurion
31 Bega (Bee)

November

1 All Saints' Day
2 Marcian (Cyrrhus)
3 Pirminus, Martin de Porres, Hubert
4 Charles Borromeo
5 Zachary, Elizabeth
6 Leonard of Noblac, Winnoc
7 Willibrord
8 Four Crowned Martyrs
9 Benignus (Benen)
10 Leo the Great, Andrew Avellino
11 Martin of Tours
12 Josaphat
13 Britius, Homobonus, Francis Xavier Cabrini
14 Lawrence O'Toole
15 Albert the Great, Fintan of Rheinau
16 Margaret of Scotland
17 Hugh of Lincoln, Gregory the Wonderworker
18 Mawes
19 Nerses I
20 Edmund
21 Albert of Louvain
22 Cecilia
23 Clement I, Columban
24 Chrysogonus
25 Catherine of Alexandria
26 John Berchmans
27 Maximus, Catherine Laboure
28 James of the March
29 Saturninus
30 Andrew

December

1 Eligius (Eloi)
2 Chromatius
3 Francis Xavier
4 Barbara, John Damascene
5 Birinus, Crispina
6 Nicholas of Bari
7 Ambrose
8 Budoc
9 Peter Fourier
10 Eulalia
11 Damasus, Corentin, Gentian
12 Jane Frances de Chantal
13 Lucy
14 John of the Cross
15 Mary di Rosa
16 Adelaide
17 Begga
18 Flannan
19 Anastasius I
20 Dominic of Silos
21 Peter Canisius
22 Chaeremon
23 John of Kanty, Thorlac
24 Delphinus
25 Anastasia, Eugenia
26 Stephen
27 John the Divine
28 The Holy Innocents
29 Thomas à Becket
30 Egwin
31 Sylvester

PATRON SAINTS OF THE UNITED KINGDOM

1 March	David of Wales
17 March	Patrick of Ireland
23 April	George of England
30 November	Andrew of Scotland

PATRON SAINTS AND INTERCESSORS

Profession, etc.	Saint	Date
Accountants	Matthew	21 September
Actors	Genesius the Comedian	25 August
Advertisers, advertising	Bernardino of Siena	20 May
Air stewards	Bona	29 May
Animals, sick	Nicholas of Tolentino	10 September
Animals, domestic	Antony the Abbot	17 January
Animals, danger from	Vitus	15 June
Apprentices	John Bosco	31 January
Archaeologists	Damasus	11 December
Archers	Sebastian	30 January
Architects	Thomas the Apostle	3 July
Armies, soldiers	Maurice	22 September
Artists	Luke	18 October
Astronauts	Joseph of Cupertino	18 September
Astronomers	Dominic	8 August
Asylums, mental	Dympna	15 May
Babies	Maximus	27 November
Bakers	Honoratus	16 May
Bankers	Matthew	21 September

Profession, etc.	Saint	Date
Barbers	Cosmas and Damian	26 September
Bee-keepers	Bernard of Clairvaux	20 August
Birds	Gall	16 October
Blacksmiths	Eligius (Eloi)	1 December
Blind people	Thomas the Apostle	3 July
Book-keepers	Matthew	21 September
Booksellers, book trade	John of God	8 March
Boys, young	Dominic Savio	9 March
Breast-feeding	Basilissa	3 September
Brewers	Amand	6 February
Bricklayers	Stephen	26 December
Brides	Nicholas of Bari	6 December
Bridges	John Nepomucen	16 May
Broadcasters	Gabriel the Archangel	29 September
Builders	Thomas the Apostle	3 July
Business people	Homobonus	13 November
Butchers	Luke	18 October
Cabinet makers	Joseph	19 March
Cake makers	Honoratus	16 May
Cancer sufferers	Peregrine Laziosi	1 May
Cemetery caretakers	Joseph of Arimathea	17 March
Charitable societies	Vincent de Paul	27 September
Chemists (pharmacists)	Cosmas and Damian	26 September
Childbirth	Raymond Nonnatus	31 August
Childless women	Anne	26 July
Children	Nicholas of Bari	6 December
Children, desire for	Rita of Cascia	22 May
Children, illegitimate	John Francis Regis	16 June
Christian people, young	Aloysius	21 June
Clergy	Gabriell Possenti	27 February

Profession, etc.	Saint	Date
Clothworkers	Homobonus	13 November
Coffin-bearers	Joseph of Arimathea	17 March
Colic	Erasmus (Elmo)	2 June
Colleges	Thomas Aquinas	28 January
Comedians	Vitus	15 June
Construction workers	Thomas the Apostle	3 July
Contagious diseases	Roch	16 August
Cooks	Lawrence	10 August
Craftsmen and -women	Eligius (Eloi)	1 December
Criminals, condemned	Dismas	25 March
Crops, protection of	Magnus of Fussen	6 September
Customs officers	Matthew	21 September
Dancers	Vitus	15 June
Deaf people	Francis de Sales	24 January
Death	Michael the Archangel	29 September
Death, happy	Joseph	19 March
Death, sudden	Andrew Avellino	10 November
Degree candidates	Joseph of Cupertino	18 September
Dentists	Apollonia	7 February
Devils, possession by	Cyriacus	8 August
Difficult situations	Eustace	20 September
Diplomatic services	Gabriel the Archangel	29 September
Disabled, physically	Giles	1 September
Disasters	Geneviève	3 January
Diseases, eye	Raphael the Archangel	29 September
Diseases, nervous	Dympna	15 May
Doctors	Luke	18 October
Dog bites	Ubald	16 May
Doubters	Joseph	19 March
Drought	Geneviève	3 January

Profession, etc.	Saint	Date
Drowning, death by or danger from	Adjutor	30 April
Dying, the	Benedict	21 March
Earthquakes	Emygdius	9 August
Ecologists, ecology	Francis of Assisi	4 October
Eczema	Antony the Abbot	17 January
Editors	John Bosco	31 January
Education	Martin de Porres	3 November
Embroiderers	Clare	11 August
Emigrants	Francis Xavier Cabrini	13 November
Engineers	Ferdinand III of Castile	30 May
Epilepsy	Dympna	15 May
Examination candidates	Joseph of Cupertino	18 September
Falsely accused people	Raymond Nonnatus	31 August
Farmers	Isidore the Farmer	15 May
Farm workers	Benedict	21 March
Fathers	Joseph	19 March
Fever	Geneviève	3 January
Fire, danger from	Agatha	5 February
Fishermen	Peter	29 June
Flood	Gregory the Wonderworker	17 NovembeR
Florists and flower growers	Rose of Lima	23 August
Flying	Joseph of Cupertino	18 September
Foresters	John Gualbert	12 July
Garage workers	Eligius (Eloi)	1 December
Gardeners	Fiacre	1 September
Girls, teenage	Maria Goretti	6 July
Glaziers	Lucy	13 December
Goldsmiths	Eligius (Eloi)	1 December
Grave-diggers	Joseph of Arimathea	17 March

Profession, etc.	Saint	Date
Grocers	Michael the Archangel	29 September
Haemorrhage	Lucy	13 December
Hairdressers	Cosmas and Damian	26 September
Harvests	Antony of Padua	13 June
Headaches	Denis, Bishop of Paris	9 October
Health inspectors	Raphael the Archangel	29 September
Hernia sufferers	Cathal	10 May
Hoarseness	Bernardino of Siena	20 May
Hopeless cases	Jude	28 October
Horses	Eligius (Eloi)	1 December
Horse-riders	Martin of Tours	11 November
Horticulturalists	Fiacre	1 September
Hospitals	John of God	8 March
Housewives	Martha	29 July
Infertility	Rita of Cascia	22 May
Innkeepers	Gentian	11 December
Insanity	Dympna	15 May
Invalids	Roch	16 August
Jewellers	Eligius (Eloi)	1 December
Joiners	Joseph	19 March
Journalists	Francis de Sales	24 January
Journeys, safe	Christopher	25 July
Judges	Ivo of Kermartin	16 May
Justice, social	Martin de Porres	3 November
Juvenile offenders	Dominic Savio	9 March
Lame people	Giles	1 September
Lawyers	Raymond of Peñafort	7 January
Learning	Catherine of Alexandria	25 November
Librarians, libraries	Jerome	30 September
Lighthouse keepers	Venerius	13 September

Profession, etc.	Saint	Date
Lightning, protection against	Magnus of Fussen	6 September
Lost articles	Antony of Padua	13 June
Lovers	Valentine	14 February
Magistrates	Ferdinand III of Castile	30 May
Mariners	Francis of Paola	2 April
Maritime pilots	Nicholas of Bari	6 December
Marriages, unhappy	Gengulf	11 May
Married women	Monica	27 August
Medical profession	Cosmas and Damian	26 September
Merchants	Homobonus	13 November
Metalworkers	Eligius (Eloi)	1 December
Midwives	Raymond Nonnatus	31 August
Migrants	Francis Xavier Cabrini	31 November
Miners	Barbara	4 December
Missions	Francis Xavier	3 December
Mothers	Monica	27 August
Motorcyclists	Mary, Our Lady of Castellazzo	Unfixed
Motorists	Frances of Rome	9 March
Mountaineers	Bernard of Montjoux	28 May
Music	Cecilia	22 November
Naval officers	Francis of Paola	2 April
Navigators	Francis of Paola	2 April
Neighbourhood watch schemes	Sebastian	20 January
Nervous diseases	Vitus	15 June
Notaries	Luke	18 October
Nurses	Camillus de Lellis	14 July
Old people	Mary, Our Lady of Consolation	20 June
Painters (artists)	Fra Angelico	18 March
Paratroopers	Michael the Archangel	29 September

Profession, etc.	Saint	Date
Parenthood	Rita of Cascia	22 May
Park keepers	John Gualbert	12 July
Pawnbrokers	Bernard of Feltre	28 September
People in authority	Ferdinand III of Castile	30 May
Pets	Antony the Abbot	17 January
Philatelists	Gabriel the Archangel	29 September
Philosophers, philosophy	Catherine of Alexandria	25 November
Pilgrims	Nicholas of Bari	6 December
Poets	Columba of Iona	9 June
Policemen and -women	Michael the Archangel	29 September
Poor people	Antony of Padua	13 June
Possession by devils	Cyriacus	8 August
Postal workers	Gabriel the Archangel	29 September
Preachers	John Chrysostom	27 January
Pregnant women	Margaret (Marina)	20 July
Priests	John Mary Vianney	4 August
Printers	John of God	8 March
Prison officers	Hippolytus	13 August
Prisoners	Leonard of Noblac	6 November
Procrastination (against)	Expeditus	19 April
Publishers	John the Divine	27 December
Quantity surveyors	Thomas the Apostle	3 July
Radio	Gabriel the Archangel	29 September
Radiologists, radiotherapists	Michael the Archangel	29 September
Rain, excessive	Geneviève	3 January
Rheumatism sufferers	James the Great	25 July
Sailors	Erasmus (Elmo)	2 June
Scholars	Thomas Aquinas	28 January
Scientists	Albert the Great	15 November
Sculptors	Luke	18 October

Profession, etc.	Saint	Date
Secretaries	Genesius the Comedian	25 August
Security forces	Michael the Archangel	29 September
Security guards	Matthew	21 September
Short-sightedness	Clarus	1 January
Shorthand writers, stenographers	Cassian of Imola	13 August
Sick people	John of God	8 March
Signals, military	Gabriel the Archangel	29 September
Silversmiths	Eligius (Eloi)	1 December
Singers	Cecilia	22 November
Skiers	Bernard of Montjoux	28 May
Skin diseases	Antony the Abbot	17 January
Slander	John Nepomucen	16 May
Sleepwalkers	Dympna	15 May
Snakebites	Pirminus	3 November
Social justice	Martin de Porres	3 November
Social workers	John Francis Regis	16 June
Soldiers	Martin of Tours	11 November
Souls in purgatory	Nicholas of Tolentino	10 September
Stomach pains	Erasmus (Elmo)	2 June
Stonemasons	Four Crowned Martyrs	8 November
Storms, protection against	Vitus	15 June
Students	Thomas Aquinas	28 January
Students, female	Catherine of Alexandria	25 November
Students, young	John Berchmans	26 November
Swimmers	Adjutor	30 April
Tailors, dressmakers	Homobonus	13 November
Tax officials	Matthew	21 September
Taxi drivers	Fiacre	1 September
Teachers	John Baptist de la Salle	7 April

Profession, etc.	Saint	Date
Telecommunications	Gabriel the Archangel	29 September
Television	Clare	11 August
Theatre	Genesius the Comedian	25 August
Theft, protection against	Dismas	25 March
Thieves, danger from	Leonard of Noblac	6 November
Throat infections	Blaise	3 February
Toothache	Apollonia	7 February
Tradesmen and -women	Homobonus	13 November
Travellers	Christopher	25 July
Undertakers	Dismas	25 March
Unmarried women	Nicholas of Bari	6 December
Urgent situations	Expeditus	19 April
Vermin, protection against	Magnus of Fussen	6 September
Veterinary surgeons	Eligius (Eloi)	1 December
Waiters, waitresses	Martha	29 July
War victims (non-combatants)	Mary, Queen of Peace	9 July
Water, danger from	Florian	4 May
Widows	Paula	26 January
Wine merchants, wine trade	Amand	6 February
Workers	Joseph	19 March
Writers	Francis de Sales	24 January
Young people	Raphael the Archangel	29 September

LARGEST RELIGIONS*

Religion	Worshippers (millions)
Christianity	1,955.2 (981 Roman Catholic, 404 Protestant, 218 Orthodox, 69 Anglican, 282 other)
Islam	1,126.3 (83% Sunnites, 16% Shi'ites, 1% other)
Hinduism	793.1 (70% Vaishnavites, 25% Shaivites)
Buddhism	325.3 (56% Mahayana, 38% Theravada, 6% Tantrayana)
Sikhism	19.5
Judaism	13.9
Confucianism	6.2
Baha'ism	5.8
Jainism	4.9
Shintoism	2.9

*Excludes tribal/folk religions and shamanism.

TYPES OF CROSS

ankh

avellane

Calvary

Celtic

cross clechée

Ansated

cross crosslet

cross fitchée

cross fleury

cross formée

cross fourchée

cross gringolée

cross moline

cross pommée

Greek

Latin

Maltese

papal

patriarchal

potent

quadrate

*St Andrew's
or Saltire*

trefled

Russian

Tau or St Anthony's

Sarcelly

Crusaders'

*Swastika or fylfot
(derived from the
pagan sunwheel)*

Cross of Lorraine

POPES OF THE ROMAN CATHOLIC CHURCH

Note: This list does not include anti-popes.

c.42	Peter	314	Sylvester I
c.67	Linus	336	Mark
c.76	Anacletus	337	Julius I
c.88	Clement I	352	Liberius
c.99	Evaristus	366	Damasus I
c.107	Alexander I	384	Siricius
c.115	Sixtus I	399	Anastasius I
c.125	Telephorus	401	Innocent I
c.136	Hyginus	417	Zosimus
c.140	Pius I	418	Boniface I
c.155	Anicetus	422	Celestine I
c.166	Soterus	432	Sixtus III
175	Eleutherius	440	Leo I (the Great)
189	Victor I	461	Hilarius
199	Zephyrinus	468	Simplicius
217	Calistus I	483	Felix III (or II)
222	Urban I	492	Gelasius I
230	Pontian	496	Anastasius II
235	Anterus	498	Symmachus
236	Fabian	514	Hormisdas
251	Cornelius	523	John I
253	Lucius I	526	Felix IV
254	Stephen I	530	Boniface II
257	Sixtus II	533	John II
259	Dionysius	535	Agapitus I
269	Felix I	536	Silverius
275	Eutychian	537	Vigilius
283	Caius	556	Pelagius II
296	Marcellinus	561	John III
308	Marcellus I	574	Benedict I
310	Eusebius	578	Pelagius II
311	Melchiades	590	Gregory I (the Great)

604	Sabinian	824	Eugenius II
607	Boniface III	827	Valentine
608	Boniface IV	827	Gregory IV
615	Deusdedit (Adeodatus I)	844	Sergius II
619	Boniface V	847	Leo IV
625	Honorius I	855	Benedict III
640	Severinus	858	Nicholas I
640	John IV	867	Adrian II
642	Theodore I	872	John VIII
649	Martin I	882	Marinus I
654	Eugenius I	884	Adrian III
657	Vitalian	885	Stephen VI
672	Adeodatus II	891	Formosus
676	Donus	896	Boniface VI
678	Agatho	896	Stephen VII
682	Leo II	897	Romanus
684	Benedict II	897	Theodore II
685	John V	898	John IX
686	Conon	900	Benedict IV
687	Sergius I	903	Leo V
701	John VI	904	Sergius III
705	John VII	911	Anastasius III
708	Sisinnius	913	Lando
708	Constantine	914	John X
715	Gregory II	928	Leo VI
731	Gregory III	928	Stephen VIII
741	Zachary	931	John XI
752	Stephen II	936	Leo VII
752	Stephen III	939	Stephen IX
757	Paul I	942	Marinus II
768	Stephen IV	946	Agapitus II
772	Adrian I	955	John XII
795	Leo III	963	Leo VIII
816	Stephen V	964	Benedict V
817	Paschal I	965	John XIII

973	Benedict VI	1181	Lucius III
974	Benedict VII	1185	Urban III
983	John XIV	1187	Gregory VIII
985	John XV	1187	Clement III
996	Gregory V	1191	Celestine III
999	Sylvester II	1198	Innocent III
1003	John XVII	1216	Honorius III
1004	John XVIII	1227	Gregory IX
1009	Sergius IV	1241	Celestine IV
1012	Benedict VIII	1243	Innocent IV
1024	John XIX	1254	Alexander IV
1032	Benedict IX	1261	Urban IV
1045	Gregory VI	1265	Clement IV
1046	Clement II	1271	Gregory X
1047	Benedict IX	1276	Innocent V
1048	Damasus II	1276	Adrian V
1049	Leo IX	1276	John XXI†
1055	Victor II	1277	Nicholas III
1057	Stephen X	1281	Martin IV
1059	Nicholas II	1285	Honorius IV
1061	Alexander II	1288	Nicholas IV
1073	Gregory VII	1294	Celestine V
1086	Victor III	1294	Boniface VIII
1088	Urban II	1303	Benedict XI
1099	Paschal II	1305	Clement V
1118	Gelasius II	1316	John XXII
1119	Callistus II	1334	Benedict XII
1124	Honorius II	1342	Clement VI
1130	Innocent II	1352	Innocent VI
1143	Celestine II	1362	Urban V
1144	Lucius II	1370	Gregory XI
1145	Eugenius III	1378	Urban VI
1153	Anastasius IV	1389	Boniface IX
1154	Adrian IV*	1404	Innocent VII
1159	Alexander III	1406	Gregory XII

1417	Martin V	1644	Innocent X
1431	Eugenius IV	1655	Alexander VII
1447	Nicholas V	1667	Clement IX
1455	Callistus III	1670	Clement X
1458	Pius II	1676	Innocent XI
1464	Paul II	1689	Alexander VIII
1471	Sixtus IV	1691	Innocent XII
1484	Innocent VIII	1700	Clement XI
1492	Alexander VI	1721	Innocent XIII
1503	Pius III	1724	Benedict XIII
1503	Julius II	1730	Clement XII
1513	Leo X	1740	Benedict XIV
1522	Adrian VI	1758	Clement XIII
1523	Clement VII	1769	Clement XIV
1534	Paul III	1775	Pius VI
1550	Julius III	1800	Pius VII
1555	Marcellus II	1823	Leo XII
1555	Paul IV	1829	Pius VIII
1559	Pius IV	1831	Gregory XVI
1566	Pius V	1846	Pius IX
1572	Gregory XIII	1878	Leo XIII
1585	Sixtus V	1903	Pius X
1590	Urban VII	1914	Benedict XV
1590	Gregory XIV	1922	Pius XI
1591	Innocent IX	1939	Pius XII
1592	Clement VIII	1958	John XXIII
1605	Leo XI	1963	Paul VI
1605	Paul V	1978	John Paul I
1621	Gregory XV	1978	John Paul II
1623	Urban VIII		

*Born Nicholas Breakspear in Abbot's Langley, Hertfordshire. The only Englishman so far to have been made Pope.
† In fact only the twentieth John but somehow an error of calculation had been made in the past.

ARCHBISHOPS OF CANTERBURY

597 Augustine	1052 Stigand
604 Laurentius	1070 Lanfranc
619 Mellitus	1093 Anselm
624 Justus	1114 Ralph d'Escures
627 Honorius	1123 William de Corbeil
655 Deusdedit	1139 Theobald
668 Theodore	1162 Thomas à Becket
692 Boerhtweald	1174 Richard (of Dover)
731 Tatwine	1185 Baldwin
735 Nothelm	1193 Hubert Walter
740 Cuthbeorht	1207 Stephen Langton
761 Breguwine	1229 Richard le Grant
765 Jaenbeorht	1234 Edmund Rich
793 Aethelheard	1245 Boniface of Savoy
805 Wulfred	1273 Robert Kilwardby
832 Feologild	1279 John Pecham
833 Ceolnoth	1294 Robert Winchelsey
870 Aethelred	1313 Walter Reynolds
890 Plegmund	1328 Simon Mepeham
914 Aethelhelm	1333 John Stratford
923 Wulfhelm	1349 Thomas Bradwardine
942 Oda	1349 Simon Islip
959 Aefsige	1366 Simon Langham
959 Beorhthelm	1368 William Whittlesey
960 Dunstan	1375 Simon Sudbury
c.988 Athelgar	1381 William Courtenay
990 Siggeric Serio	1396 Thomas Arundel
995 Aelfric	1398 Roger Walden
1005 Aelfheah	1414 Henry Chichele
1013 Lyfing	1443 John Strafford
1020 Aethelnoth	1452 John Kemp
1038 Eadsige	1454 Thomas Bourchier
1051 Robert of Jumièges	1486 John Morton

1501	Henry Dean
1503	William Warham
1533	Thomas Cranmer*
1556	Reginald Pole
1559	Matthew Parker
1576	Edmund Grindal
1583	John Whitgift
1604	Richard Bancroft
1611	George Abbot
1633	William Laud
1660	William Juxon
1663	Gilbert Sheldon
1678	William Sancroft
1691	John Tillotson
1695	Thomas Tenison
1716	William Wake
1737	John Potter
1747	Thomas Herring
1757	Matthew Hutton
1758	Thomas Secker
1768	Frederick Cornwallis
1783	John Moore
1805	Charles Manners Sutton
1828	William Howley
1848	John Bird Sumner
1862	Charles Thomas Longley
1868	Archibald Campbell Tait
1883	Edward White Benson
1896	Frederick Temple
1903	Randall Thomas Davidson
1928	Cosmo Gordon Lang
1942	William Temple
1945	Geoffrey Francis Fisher
1961	Arthur Michael Ramsey
1974	Frederick Donald Coggan
1980	Robert Alexander Kennedy Runcie
1991	George Leonard Carey

Supported Henry VIII in his claims to be supreme head of the Church of England, thus severing links with Rome. Condemned for heresy in Queen Mary's reign and burned at the stake in Oxford in 1556.

BOOKS OF THE BIBLE

Protestant Canon Old Testament	Roman Catholic Canon Old Testament
Genesis	Genesis
Exodus	Exodus
Leviticus	Leviticus
Numbers	Numbers
Deuteronomy	Deuteronomy
Joshua	Joshua (Josue)
Judges	Judges
Ruth	Ruth
1 Samuel	1 Samuel (1 Kings)
2 Samuel	2 Samuel (2 Kings)
1 Kings	1 Kings (3 Kings)
2 Kings	2 Kings (4 Kings)
1 Chronicles	1 Chronicles (1 Paralipomenon)
2 Chronicles	2 Chronicles (2 Paralipomenon)
Ezra	Ezra (1 Esdras)
Nehemiah	Nehemiah (2 Esdras)
	Tobit (Tobias)
	Judith
Esther	Esther
Job	Job
Psalms	Psalms
	Proverbs
Ecclesiastes	Ecclesiastes
Song of Solomon	Song of Solomon (Canticle of Canticles)
	The Wisdom of Solomon (Wisdom)

Protestant Canon
Old Testament cont.

Isaiah
Jeremiah
Lamentations

Ezekiel
Daniel
Hosea
Joel
Amos
Obadiah
Jonah
Micah
Nahum
Habakkuk
Zephaniah
Haggai
Zechariah
Malachi

Roman Catholic Canon
Old Testament cont.
Sirach (Ecclesiasticus)
Isaiah
Jeremiah
Lamentations
Baruch
Ezekiel (Ezechiel)
Daniel
Hosea (Osee)
Joel
Amos
Obadiah (Abdias)
Jonah (Jonas)
Micah (Micheas)
Nahum
Habakkuk (Habacuc)
Zephaniah (Sophonias)
Haggai (Aggeus)
Zechariah (Zacharias)
Malachi (Malachias)
1 Maccabees
(1 Machabees)
2 Maccabees
(2 Machabees)

Protestant Canon
New Testament
Matthew
Mark
Luke
John

Roman Catholic Canon
New Testament
Matthew
Mark
Luke
John

Protestant Canon	**Roman Catholic Canon**
New Testament *cont.*	**New Testament** *cont.*
The Acts of the Apostles	The Acts of the Apostles
Romans	Romans
1 Corinthians	1 Corinthians
2 Corinthians	2 Corinthians
Galatians	Galatians
Ephesians	Ephesians
Philippians	Philippians
Colossians	Colossians
1 Thessalonians	1 Thessalonians
2 Thessalonians	2 Thessalonians
1 Timothy	1 Timothy
2 Timothy	2 Timothy
Titus	Titus
Philemon	Philemon
Hebrews	Hebrews
James	James
1 Peter	1 Peter
2 Peter	2 Peter
1 John	1 John
2 John	2 John
3 John	3 John
Jude	Jude
Revelation	Revelation (Apocalypse)

Protestant Canon	**Roman Catholic Canon**
Apocrypha	**Apocrypha**
The First Book of Esdras	1 (3) Esdras
The Second Book of Esdras	2 (4) Esdras
Tobit	Tobit

Protestant Canon	Roman Catholic Canon
Apocrypha *cont.*	**Apocrypha** *cont.*
Judith	Judith
The Rest of the Chapters of the Book of Esther	Additions to Esther
The Wisdom of Solomon	The Wisdom of Solomon
Ecclesiasticus or the Wisdom of Jesus, Son of Sirach	Sirach
Baruch	Baruch
A Letter of Jeremiah	The Letter of Jeremiah
The Song of the Three Holy Children	The Prayer of Azariah and the Song of the Three Young Men
Daniel and Susanna	Susanna
Daniel, Bel and the Snake	Bel and the Dragon
The Prayer of Manasseh	The Prayer of Manasseh
The First Book of the Maccabees	1 Maccabees
The Second Book of the Maccabees	2 Maccabees

JEWISH TEXTS

The Law (Pentateuch)	The Prophets	The Writings
Genesis	Joshua	Psalms
Exodus	Judges	Proverbs
Leviticus	Samuel	Job
Numbers	Kings	Song of Solomon
Deuteronomy	Isaiah	Ruth
	Jeremiah	Lamentations

The Law (Pentateuch)	The Prophets	The Writings
	Ezekiel	Malachi
	Hosea	Ecclesiastes
	Joel	Esther
	Amos	Daniel
	Obadiah	Ezra
	Jonah	Nehemiah
	Micah	Chronicles
	Nahum	
	Habakkuk	
	Zephaniah	
	Haggai	
	Zechariah	

THE KORAN

Chapters of the Koran.

1 Entitled, The Preface or Introduction
2 Entitled, The Cow
3 Entitled, The Family of Imran
4 Entitled, Women
5 Entitled, The Table
6 Entitled, Cattle
7 Entitled, Al Araf
8 Entitled, The Spoils
9 Entitled, The Declaration of Immunity
10 Entitled, Jonas
11 Entitled, Hud
12 Entitled, Joseph
13 Entitled, Thunder
14 Entitled, Abraham
15 Entitled, Al Hejr
16 Entitled, The Bee
17 Entitled, The Night Journey
18 Entitled, The Cave
19 Entitled, Mary
20 Entitled, T.H.
21 Entitled, The Prophets

22 Entitled, The Pilgrimage
23 Entitled, The True Believers
24 Entitled, Light
25 Entitled, Al Forkan
26 Entitled, The Poets
27 Entitled, The Ant
28 Entitled, The Story
29 Entitled, The Spider
30 Entitled, The Greeks
31 Entitled, Lokman
32 Entitled, Adoration
33 Entitled, The Confederates
34 Entitled, Saba
35 Entitled, The Creator
36 Entitled, Y.S.
37 Entitled, Those who Rank themselves in Order
38 Entitled, S.
39 Entitled, The Troops
40 Entitled, The True Believer
41 Entitled, Are Distinctly Explained
42 Entitled, Consultation
43 Entitled, The Ornaments of Gold
44 Entitled, Smoke
45 Entitled, The Kneeling
46 Entitled, Al Ahkaf
47 Entitled, Mohammed
48 Entitled, The Victory
49 Entitled, The Inner Apartments
50 Entitled, K.
51 Entitled, The Dispersing
52 Entitled, The Mountain
53 Entitled, The Star
54 Entitled, The Moon
55 Entitled, The Merciful
56 Entitled, The Inevitable
57 Entitled, Iron
58 Entitled, She who Disputed
59 Entitled, The Emigration
60 Entitled, She who is Tied
61 Entitled, Battle Array
62 Entitled, The Assembly
63 Entitled, The Hypocrites
64 Entitled, Mutual Deceit
65 Entitled, Divorce
66 Entitled, Prohibition
67 Entitled, The Kingdom
68 Entitled, The Pen
69 Entitled, The Infallible
70 Entitled, The Steps
71 Entitled, Noah
72 Entitled, The Genii
73 Entitled, The Wrapped Up
74 Entitled, The Covered
75 Entitled, The Resurrection

HINDU TEXTS

Hinduism has no single volume representing its doctrines. Of the many sacred writings which go to make up its fundamental beliefs, the following are considered to be the most significant:

The Vedas:

Rig-Veda	Yajur-Veda
Sama-Veda	Atharva-Veda

The Puranas:
Ramayana
Mahabharata (including the Bhagavadgita)
The Manu Smriti (Code of Manu)

BUDDHIST (PALI) TEXTS

1 **Canonical Literature**
   The Three Baskets of Tripitaka
   Vinaya Pitaka – Basket of Discipline
   Sutta Pitaka – Basket of Discourses
   Abhidharma Pitaka – Basket of the Higher Dharma

Note: Additional scriptures have been added by the various Buddhist schools.

2 **Non-canonical Literature**
a **Chronicles**
   Dipavamsa – 'Island Chronicle'
   Mahavamsa – 'Great Chronicle'
   Culavamsa – 'Little Chronicle'
   Mahabodhivamsa – 'Chronicle of the Bodhi-Tree'

Thupavamsa – 'Chronicle of the Stupa'

Daathavamsa – 'Chronicle of the Sacred Relic' (i.e. the Buddha's tooth)

Sasanavamsa – 'Chronicle of the Religion'

b Commentaries on Canonical Texts

These are too numerous to list, but among the most important are those composed by Buddhaghosa on the Vinaya Pitaka, the Digha Nikaya and on the first book of the Abhidharma Pitaka.

c Compendiums or manuals of Buddhist life and philosophy based on Canonical Texts

Again, too numerous to list but works such as the Visuddhimagga, the Malindapanha and the Abhidhammatthasangaha are the most important.

PRINCIPAL GODS

GREEK

Name of Deity	Representing/symbolizing
Zeus	God of gods
Poseidon	The sea; father of rivers and fountains
Hades	The underworld; death
Apollo	The sun
Hermes	Messenger and herald of the gods
Ares	War
Hephaestus	Fire
Dionysus	Wine
Uranus	Heaven
Hera	Goddess of the heavens; patroness and protector of marriage
Demeter	Abundance of corn and fruit; agriculture
Hestia	Hearth and home
Artemis	Moon, hunting, chastity
Athene	Wisdom

Greek *cont.*

Name of Deity	Representing/symbolizing
Aphrodite	Love and beauty
Hebe	Youth
Gaea	Earth

ROMAN

Name of Deity	Representing/symbolizing
Jupiter	God of gods
Neptune	The sea
Pluto	The underworld; death
Apollo	The sun
Mercury	Messenger of the gods
Mars	War
Vulcan	Fire
Bacchus	Wine
Coelus	Heaven
Saturn	Abundance
Juno	Queen of the heavens; guardian of women
Ceres	Agriculture
Vesta	Hearth and home
Diana	Hunting; chastity
Minerva	Wisdom
Venus	Love; beauty
Terra	Earth

Note: Saturn's day = Saturday

NORSE

Name of Deity	Representing/symbolizing
Odin	Chief god; war, wisdom, poetry, prophecy, magic
Thor	Thunder
Balder	Sun
Hermod	Messenger of the gods

Norse cont.

Name of Deity	Representing/symbolizing
Tyr	War; athletic activities. A hero, the killer of Game, the Hellhound
Forseti	Guardian of justice
Bragi	Poetry, wisdom and eloquence; welcomed dead warriors to the underworld
Heimdal	Light; guardian of the Bifrost, the rainbow bridge leading to Valhalla
Hodur	Blind son of Odin; god of night
Vidar	Forests; 'the silent god'
Uller	Hunting
Vali	Son of Odin
Thjazi	Winter
Holler	Death
Mimir	Custodian of the Fountain of Wisdom
Ymir	Frost giant
Kari	Son of Ymir; controls air, storms
Hler	Son of Ymir; controls the sea
Logi	Son of Ymir; controls fire
Aegir	Giant of the seashore
Frey	Fruitfulness; sender of sunshine and rain
Frigga	Earth, air, conjugal love
Fulla	Mother goddess
Sjofna	Love
Lofn	Reconciliation of separated lovers
Vara	Punishment of unfaithful lovers
Syn	One of Frigga's attendants
Gerda	The frozen earth
Freyja	Fertility, love
Jord	Earth
Saga	History
Iduna	Spring; guardian of the apples which rejuvenated the gods

Norse *cont.*

Name of Deity	Representing/symbolizing
Bil	Child-deity; associated with waning moon
Siguna	Truth
Nanna	Wife of Balder; possessor of magic ring
Gefjon	Protection of girls who died unmarried
Snotra	Wisdom
Gna	Messenger of the goddesses
Hel	The dead
Eir	Healing
Ran	Storms and the sea; drew the drowned under the waves in her net

Note: Odin's day (Anglo-Saxon 'Woden') = Wednesday; Thor's day = Thursday; Freyja's day = Friday

Other Figures

The three Norns represent Fate: Urda represents the past, Verdandi the present and Skuld the future. The thirteen Valkyries rode through the air and over the sea to select those who were to die in battle and whose souls were then transported to Valhalla where they enjoyed a perfect and everlasting existence, feasting and recounting their deeds of valour.

The elves were tiny creatures who plagued or helped mankind according to whim. The dwarfs lived in the heart of the hills and were metalworkers and jewellers. The giants stole summer and brought winter in its place. One of these was Hresvelgr who produced winds and storms by moving his wings.

EGYPTIAN

Name of Deity	Representing/symbolizing
Osiris	Earth, sky; principle of good
Set	Darkness; principle of evil
Ra	Sun
Shu	Dry atmospheres
Tefnut	Waters above the heavens
Name of Deity	Representing/symbolizing
Keb	Earth, vegetation
Pthah	Artisan of the world (made sun, moon, earth); holds world in his hands
Horus	Light
Anubis	The dead; art of embalming
Thoth	Art of letters; registrar and recorder of the underworld
Apis	Beast-god in form of a bull
Khem	Generation and production
Ranno	Gardens
Serapis	Healing
Isis	Earth, moon; has limitless powers
Maut	Mother of gods; mistress of sky
Athor	Sky, rising and setting sun; love and beauty
Maat	Truth; law and order
Mu	Light
Nephthys	The dead; personification of dusk
Neith	Upper heaven or ether
Anouke	War
Babastis	Gentle rays of the sun
Sekhet	Burning heat of the sun
Sphinx	Wisdom; earth's abundance
Anquet	Fertilizing waters of the Nile
Nut	Childbirth; nursing

Science

GEOLOGICAL TABLE

Era	Period	Epoch	Time	Major Events	Animal and Plant Life
Cenozoic		Quaternary		Holocene (recent)	c.0.01
				Pleistocene	c.2
		Tertiary		Pliocene	c.5
				Miocene	25
				Oligocene	40
				Eocene	55
				Palaeocene	65
Mesozoic		Cretaceous			135
		Jurassic			200
		Triassic			250
Palaeozoic		Permean			290
		Carboniferous			350
		Devonian			400
		Silurian			440
		Ordovician			500
		Cambrian			600
Precambrian		Proterozoic			2500
		Archaeozoic			3000
		Azoic			4000
					4500

Ages in millions of years (estimated).

Ice Ages affect N Hemisphere temperature; sea retreats	End of Ice Age development of man; vegetation – Arctic forms to present form
Shallow seas in Europe	Mammals spread, early man
Thick unconsolidated clays	Whales and apes
Deposits on Great Plains	Modern mammals
Alpine-Himalayan mountain building	First horses, elephants
	Early mammals
Chalk deposited in deep seas over Europe and Asia; marginal seas in N America	End of dinosaurs, flowering plants spread
Deep sea in Europe, swamps in N America	Giant dinosaurs, first birds
W Europe – shallow sea, red sands in N America	Small dinosaurs, first mammals
Shallow seas, continental deposits, mountain building	
Shallow seas over continents, extensive mountain building, coal formation	Forests formed coal, first reptiles
Erosion, large shallow seas, sandstones, thick shales	First forests and land animals, amphibians
Erosion, low areas resubmerged, mountain building in N America, Europe and Siberia	First land plants
Europe and N America mainly submerged; continental uplift	First fishes
Europe mainly submerged; N America submerged with large shallow areas	
	Sea animals without backbones, seaweeds
	First primitive plants and animals
	Earliest known rocks
	Earth formed

CHEMICAL ELEMENTS

Name	Atomic Number	Symbol	Atomic Weight
Actinium	89	Ac	227.0278*
Aluminium	13	Al	26.98154
Americium	95	Am	243.0614*
Antimony	51	Sb	121.75
Argon	18	Ar	39.948
Arsenic	33	As	74.9216
Astatine	85	At	209.9870*
Barium	56	Ba	137.33
Berkelium	97	Bk	247.0703*
Beryllium	4	Be	9.01218
Bismuth	83	Bi	208.9804
Bohrium	107	Bh	262.1229*
Boron	5	B	10.81
Bromine	35	Br	79.904
Cadmium	48	Cd	112.41
Caesium	55	Cs	132.9054
Calcium	20	Ca	40.08
Californium	98	Cf	251.0796*
Carbon	6	C	12.011
Cerium	58	Ce	140.12
Chlorine	17	Cl	35.453
Chromium	24	Cr	51.996
Cobalt	27	Co	58.9332
Copper	29	Cu	63.546
Curium	96	Cm	247.703*
Dubnium	105	Db	261.1087*
Dysprosium	66	Dy	162.5
Einsteinium	99	Es	254.0880*

Name	Atomic Number	Symbol	Atomic Weight
Erbium	68	Er	167.26
Europium	63	Eu	151.96
Fermium	100	Fm	257.0951*
Fluorine	9	F	18.9984*
Francium	87	Fr	223.0197*
Gallium	31	Ga	69.72
Gadolinium	64	Gd	157.25
Germanium	32	Ge	72.59
Gold	79	Au	196.9665
Hafnium	72	Hf	178.49
Hassium†	108	Hs	265.1302
Helium	2	He	4.0026
Holmium	67	Ho	164.9304
Hydrogen	1	H	1.0079
Iodine	53	I	126.9045
Indium	49	In	114.82
Iridium	77	Ir	192.22
Iron	26	Fe	55.847
Krypton	36	Kr	83.8
Lanthanum	57	La	138.9055
Lawrencium	103	Lr	260.105*
Lead	82	Pb	207.19
Lithium	3	Li	6.941
Lutetium	71	Lu	174.97
Magnesium	12	Mg	24.305
Manganese	25	Mn	54.938
Meitnerium	109	Mt	266.1376*
Mendelevium	101	Md	258.099*
Mercury	80	Hg	200.59
Molybdenum	42	Mo	95.94

Name	Atomic Number	Symbol	Atomic Weight
Neodymium	60	Nd	144.24
Neon	10	Ne	20.179
Neptunium	93	Np	237.0482*
Nickel	28	Ni	58.71
Niobium	41	Nb	92.9064
Nitrogen	7	N	14.0067
Nobelium	102	No	259.101*
Oxygen	8	O	15.9994
Osmium	76	Os	190.2
Palladium	46	Pd	106.4
Phosphorus	15	P	30.97376
Platinum	78	Pt	195.09
Plutonium	94	Pu	244.0642*
Polonium	84	Po	208.9824*
Potassium	19	K	39.0983
Praseodymium	59	Pr	140.9077
Promethium	61	Pm	144.9128*
Protactinium	91	Pa	231.0359
Radium	88	Ra	226.0254*
Radon	86	Rn	222.0176*
Rhenium	75	Re	186.207
Rhodium	45	Rh	102.9055
Rubidium	37	Rb	85.4678
Ruthenium	44	Ru	101.07
Rutherfordium	104	Ru	261
Samarium	62	Sm	150.35
Scandium	21	Sc	44.9559
Seaborgium†	106	Sg	263.1182*
Selenium	34	Se	78.96
Sodium	11	Na	22.98977

Name	Atomic Number	Symbol	Atomic Weight
Silicon	14	Si	28.0855
Silver	47	Ag	107.868
Strontium	38	Sr	87.62
Sulphur	16	S	32.064
Tantalum	73	Ta	180.9479
Technetium	43	Tc	96.9064*
Tellurium	52	Te	127.6
Terbium	65	Tb	158.9254
Thallium	81	Tl	204.37
Thorium	90	Th	232.0381
Thulium	69	Tm	168.9342
Tin	50	Sn	118.69
Titanium	22	Ti	47.9
Tungsten	74	W	183.85
Ununbium†	112	Uub	277
Ununnilium†	110	Uun	269
Unununium†	111	Uuu	272
Uranium	92	U	238.029*
Vanadium	23	V	50.9414
Xenon	54	Xe	131.3
Ytterbium	70	Yb	173.04
Yttrium	39	Y	88.9059
Zinc	30	Zn	65.381
Zirconium	40	Zr	91.22

*The atomic weight of the isotope with the longest known half-life.
† Names being reviewed by the International Union of Pure and Applied Chemistry (IUPAC).

PERIODIC TABLE

Calcium, gold and hydrogen are chemical elements which are examples of basic chemical substances. They cannot be broken down into simpler forms. This gives each element distinctive properties. The periodic table gives information about all the 112 known elements. (Elements 104 to 112 have been produced artificially.)

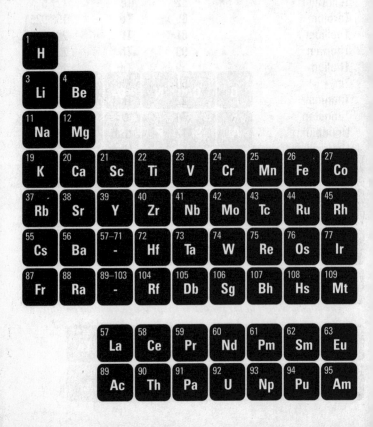

The periodic table was devised in 1869 by the Russian chemist Dmitri Mendeleyev. The table groups elements into seven lines or periods. As we read from left to right the elements become less metallic. The elements in each vertical group have similar chemical properties. Further information about the elements is given on pages 132–135.

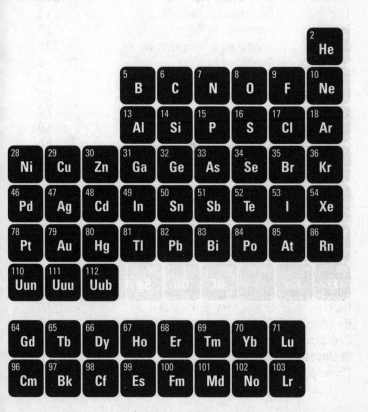

MOHS' HARDNESS SCALE

This scale was invented by Friedrich Mohs (1773–1839), a German mineralogist, and is used for testing the hardness of materials by comparing them with the ten standard minerals.

Mineral	Simple hardness test	Mohs' Hardness
Talc	Crushed by fingernail	1.0
Gypsum	Scratched by fingernail	2.0
Calcite	Scratched by copper coin	3.0
Fluorspar	Scratched by glass	4.0
Apatite	Scratched by a penknife	5.0
Feldspar	Scratched by quartz	6.0
Quartz	Scratched by a steel file	7.0
Topaz	Scratched by corundum	8.0
Corundum	Scratched by a diamond	9.0
Diamond		10.0

Gemstones

Mineral	Colour	Mohs' Hardness
Agate	Brown, red, blue, green, yellow	7.0
Alexandrite	Green	7.5
Amethyst	Violet	7.0
Aquamarine	Sky blue, greenish blue	7.5
Beryl	Green, blue, pink	7.5
Bloodstone	Green with red spots	7.0
Carnelian	Red, reddish-yellow	7.0
Chalcedony	All colours	7.0
Chrysoprase	Apple green	7.0

Mineral	Colour	Mohs' Hardness
Citrine	Yellow	7.0
Diamond	Colourless; tints of various colours	10.0
Emerald	Green	7.5
Garnet	Red and other colours	6.5-7.25
Jade	Green, whitish, mauve, brown	7.0
Lapis lazuli	Deep blue	5.5
Malachite	Dark green banded	3.5
Moonstone	Whitish with blue shimmer	6.0
Onyx	Various colours with straight coloured bands	7.0
Opal	Black, white, orange-red, rainbow	6.0
Pearl	Pale greyish-white, black	–
Peridot	Pale green	–
Ruby	Red	9.0
Sapphire	Blue and other colours	9.0
Sardonyx	Reddish brown, white bands	7.0
Serpentine	Red and green	3.0
Soapstone	White, possibly marked by impurities	2.0
Sunstone	Whitish-reddish-brown with golden particles	6.0
Topaz	Blue, green, pink, yellow, colourless	8.0
Tourmaline	Brown-black, blue, pink, red, violet-red, yellow, green	7.5
Turquoise	Greenish-grey, sky blue	6.0
Zircon	All colours	7.5

SCIENTIFIC LAWS

Physics – Gases

Scientist	Dates
Boyle, Robert	1627–91
Charles, Jacques	1746–1823
Dalton, John	1766–1844
Henry, William	1774–1836
Avogadro, Amedeo	1776–1856
Gay-Lussac, Joseph Louis	1778–1850
Graham, Thomas	1805–69

Physics – Fluids

Scientist	Dates
Archimedes	287–212 BC
Pascal, Blaise	1623–62

Description

The volume of a given mass of gas is inversely proportional to its pressure, temperature remaining constant.

The volume of a given mass of gas is directly proportional to its absolute temperature, pressure remaining constant.

Law of Partial Pressures. In a mixture of gases, the pressure of a component gas is the same as if it alone occupied the space. Atomic Theory. Elements are composed of atoms that can combine in definite proportions to form compounds.

The weight of gas dissolved by a liquid is proportional to the gas pressure.

Equal volumes of all gases at the same temperature contain the same quantity of molecules.

When gases react, they do so in volumes which bear a simple ratio to one another and to the volume of the product if it is a gas, temperature and pressure remaining constant.

The rates of diffusion of gases are inversely proportional to the square roots of their densities.

Description

Principle of Displacement. When a body is totally or partially immersed in a fluid it experiences an upthrust equal to the weight of the fluid displaced. Principle of Flotation. When a body floats it displaces a weight of fluid equal to its own weight.

In a fluid, pressure applied at any point is transmitted equally throughout it.

| Bernoulli, Daniel | 1700–82 |
| Blagden, Charles | 1748-1820 |

Physics – Energy

Scientist	Dates
Hooke, Robert	1635–1703
Ohm, Georg Simon	1787–1854
Faraday, Michael	1791–1867
Doppler, Christian	1803–53
Lenz, H F E	1804–65
Planck, Max	1858–1947

Physics – Relativity

Scientist	Dates
Einstein, Albert	1879–1955

When the speed of a fluid increases the pressure in the fluid decreases, and when speed decreases pressure increases.

At constant pressure and for dilute solutions, the elevation of boiling point or the depression of freezing point of the solvent is directly proportional to the concentration of a given solute.

Description

The extension produced in a spring is proportional to the applied force.

Voltage (V) in volts between ends of a conductor equals product of current (I) in amps flowing through it and its resistance (R): $V=IR$

1. The mass of a given element liberated during electrolysis is directly proportional to the magnitude of the steady current used to the time for which the current passes.
2. The masses of different elements liberated by the same quantity of electricity are directly proportional to their chemical equivalents.

The apparent change in frequency of sound or light caused by movement of a source with respect to the observer.

When a wire moves in a magnetic field, the electric current induced in the wire generates a magnetic field that tends to oppose the movement.

Quantum Theory. Light and other forms of energy are given off as separate packets (quanta) of energy.

Description

Theory of Relativity. Mass and energy are related by the equation $E=mc^2$, where E is the energy produced by a mass change m, and c is the speed of light.

Physics – Motion

Scientist	Dates
Newton, Sir Isaac	1642–1727

Chemistry

Scientist	Dates
Le Chatelier, H L	1850–1936

Mathematics

Scientist	Dates
Pythagoras	580–500 BC

Description

Laws of Motion:
1. A body will continue in its state of rest or uniform velocity unless acted on by an unbalanced force.
2. The rate of change of momentum of a body varies directly to the force causing the change and takes place in the same direction as the force.
3. If a body A exerts a force F on a body B then B exerts a force -F on A; that is, action and reaction are equal and opposite.
4. If no external force acts on a system in a particular direction then the total momentum of the system in that direction remains unchanged.
Law of Gravitation. The force of the attraction between two given particles is inversely proportional to the square of their distance apart.

Description

If a system in chemical equilibrium is subjected to a disturbance it tends to change in a way which opposes the disturbance.

Description

In a right-angled triangle, the square on the longest side (the hypotenuse) is equal to the sum of the squares on the other two sides.

INVENTIONS

Invention/Discovery	Year	Name and/or Country
Aeroplane	1903	Orville and Wilbur Wright
Aerosol can	1926	Erik Rotheim
Airship, rigid	1906	Ferdinand von Zeppelin
Anemometer	1644	Robert Hooke
Aspirin	1899	Felix Hoffmann
Atomic bomb	1945	Frisch, Bohr, Peierls
Bakelite	1907	Leo Baekeland
Balloon	1783	Joseph and Etienne Montgolfier
Barometer	1643	Evangelista Torricelli
Battery, electric	c.1799	Volta and Galvani
Bicycle	1839	Kirkpatrick Macmillan
Calculator, pocket	1971	Kilby, van Tassell, Merryman
Camera obscura	1560	Giovanni Battista della Porta
Canning, food	1810	Nicholas Appert
Canning, petfood	1865	James Spratt
Car, diesel	1895	Rudolf Diesel
Car, fuel-cell powered	1996	Daimler-Benz
Car, gas	1807	Isaac de Rivez
Car, internal combustion engine	1884	Gottlieb Daimler
Car, petrol engine	1886	Karl Benz
Cats' eyes	1934	Percy Shaw
Cellophane	1908	J.E. Brandenburger
Centigrade scale	c.1741	Anders Celsius
Chloroform	1847	James Young Simpson
Choc-ice	1922	C.K. Nelson
Christmas card	1843	John Calcott Horsley
Coca Cola	1886	John Pemberton
Cocoa powder	1828	Conraad Johannes van Houten
Coinage	650-600 BC	Asia Minor
Coffee, instant	1937	Nestlé
Compact disc	1979	Philips, Sony

Invention/Discovery	Year	Name and/or Country
Compact disc interactive player	1992	Philips
Compass	1269	Petrus Peregrinus de Maricourt (some authorities cite China c.1000/1100)
Computer, electronic	1948	Frederick Williams
Computer, personal	1981	IBM
Concorde supersonic aeroplane	1969	Britain/France
Concrete	133 BC	Romans
Contact lens	1887	Eugen A. Frick
Contact lens (plastic corneal lens)	1956	Norman Bier
Contraceptive, oral	1956	Gregory Pincus (first large-scale experiments)
Cornflakes	1894	J. & W. Kellogg
Credit card	1950	Ralph Schneider
Crossbow	400 BC	China
Crossword puzzle	1913	Arthur Wynne
Dictionary	600 BC	Mesopotamia (written in Akkadian)
Disc brake	1902	Frederick Lanchester
Doll, talking	1823	Johann Maelzel
Dye, hair	1909	Eugene Schueller
Dye, synthetic	1856	William H. Perkin
Dynamite	1866	Alfred Nobel
Dynamo	1871	Zénobe Gramme
Elastoplast	1928	Smith & Nephew Ltd
Electrocardiograph	1903	Wilhelm Einthoven
Engine, jet	1937	Frank Whittle
Escalator	1892	Reno and Wheeler
Fan, rotary	180	China
Film, photographic	1888	George Eastman
Fire extinguisher	1762	Dr Godfrey (also attrib. to George Manby, 1816)
Geiger counter	1913	Rutherford and Geiger
Gimbals	180	China

Invention/Discovery	Year	Name and/or Country
Glassmaking	1500 BC	Mesopotamia
Gramophone record	1887	Emile Berliner
Gun, machine (flintlock)	1718	James Puckle
Gunpowder	221 BC	China
Handkerchiefs, disposable	1924	Kimberley Clark Co
Helicopter	1907	Louis and Jacques Breguet
Hovercraft	1959	Christopher Cockerell
Inflatable swimming aid	880 BC	King Assur-Nasir Apli II of Assyria
Ink	2500 BC	China
Insulin	1921	Discovered by Paulesco
Iron, domestic steam	1938	Edmund Schreyer
Iron, electric	1882	Henry W. Seeley
Kaleidoscope	1816	David Brewster
Kirby hairgrip	1893	Hindes
Kite	400 BC	China
Lamp, halogen	1980	Philips
Laser	1960	Charles Townes
Lawnmower	1831	Edward Budding , design; Ferrabee, manufacture
Lego	1955	Ole and Godtfried Kirk Christiansen
Lightbulb	1877	Edison and Swan
Lighthouse	285 BC	Pharos, near Alexandria
Lightning conductor	1752	Benjamin Franklin
Locomotive, diesel	1912	Sulzer Co
Locomotive, steam	1804	Richard Trevithick
Loudspeaker	1924	Rice-Kellogg
Magnifying glass	1250	Roger Bacon
Margarine	1869	Hippolyte Mège-Mouriés
Mars bar	1920	Frank Mars
Meccano	1900	Frank Hornby
Metal detector	1931	Gerhard Fisher
Meteorological map	1686	Edmund Halley
Microchip	1959	Kilby and Robert Noyce
Micrometer	1638	William Gascoigne
Microprocessor	1971	Intel Corporation

Invention/Discovery	Year	Name and/or Country
Microphone	1878	David Edward Hughes
Microscope, compound	1590	Hans and Zacharias Janssen
Milking machine	1862	L.O. Colvin
Monopoly	1933	Charles Darrow
Motorcycle	1885	Gottlieb Daimler
Neon lighting	c.1910	Georges Claude
Nivea creme	1911	Paul Beiersdorf
Nylon	1937	Wallace Carruthers
Ovaltine	1904	George Wander
Oven, microwave	1945	Percy le Baron Spencer
Pacemaker, cardiac	1958	Ake Senning
Padlock	c.1380	Inventor unknown
Pan, non- stick	1954	Marc Gregoire
Paper, toilet	1857	Joseph Cayetty
Paper, writing	100	Cai Lun
Paperclip	1900	Johann Waaler
Parachute	1797	André Jacques Garnerin
Parking meter	1935	Carlton C. Magee
Pen, ballpoint	1938	Laszlo and George Biro
Pen, fibre tip	1963	Pentel Co.
Pen, fountain	1884	Lewis Edson Waterman
Penicillin	1928	Alexander Fleming
Pentium 64-bit processor	1993	Intel Co.
Perspex	1934	Rowland Hill
Photography (metal)	1826	Joseph Niépce
Photography (paper)	1835	William Fox Talbot
Pistol	1540	Camillo Vettelli
Post-it notes	1981	Spencer Sylver
Pressure cooker	1680	Denis Papin
Printing (clay characters)	1041	Bi Shang
Printing (movable type)	1447	Johannes Gensfleisch zur Laden zum Gutenberg
Pump, steam	1698	Thomas Savery
Radar	1922	A. Taylor and L. Young

Invention/Discovery	Year	Name and/or Country
Radiator	1897	Wilhelm Maybach
Radio	1901	Guglielmo Marconi
Radio broadcast (public)	1906	Reginald Aubrey Fessenden
Recorder, video	1956	Ampex Corporation
Refrigerator	1862	James Harrison
Revolver	1835	Samuel Colt
Rifle barrel	1520	August Kotter
Saccharine	1879	Constantin Fahlberg
Safety lamp, miner's	1816	Humphry Davy
Safety pin	1849	Walter Hunt
Scotch tape	1925	Richard Drew, US; introduced to UK from France as Sellotape
Scrabble	1948	James Brunot
Seat belt, car	1903	Gustave Desiré Liebau
Secateurs	1815	Bertrand de Moleville
Sewer, city	600 BC	Cloaca Maxima, Rome
Sewing machine	1830	Barthélemy Thimonnier
Sextant	1757	John Campbell
Soda-water maker	1820	Charles Cameron
Spark plug	1885	Etienne Lenoir
Spectacles	1281	Salvino degli Armati and Alessandro della Spina
Spinning Jenny	1768	Thomas Higgs; perfected by James Hargreaves
Spirit level	1662	Jean de Melchisedech Thevenot
Stainless steel	1913	Harry Brearley
Stapler	1868	Charles Henry Gould
Submarine	1776	David Bushnell
Tape recorder	1935	AEG GmbH
Tea bags	1919	Joseph Krieger
Teddy bear	1902	Morris Mitcham and Richard Steiff
Telegraph, electric	1830	Samuel Morse
Telegraph, transatlantic	1866	William Thompson
Telephone	1876	Alexander Graham Bell

Invention/Discovery	Year	Name and/or Country
Telescope	1608	Hans Lippershey; perfected by Galileo Galilei in 1609
Telescope, reflecting	1672	Isaac Newton
Television	1926	Baird, Scotland; Jenkins, US; Mihaly, Germany
Theodolite	1787	Jesse Ramsden
Thermometer, mercury	1714	Gabriel Fahrenheit
Thimble	1684	Nicholas van Benschoten
Toaster, pop-up	1927	Charles Strite
Toilet, flush	1589	John Harington
Toothbrush	1498	China
Train, high-speed (TGV)	1978	France
Tram	1775	John Outram
Transistor	1947	Shockley, Bardeen, Brattain
Tuning fork	1711	John Shore
Tupperware	1945	Earl W. Tupper
Typewriter	1808	Pelegrino Turri
Tyre, pneumatic	1888	John Boyd Dunlop
Vacuum cleaner	1869	Ives W. McGaffey (also attrib. to H.C. Booth, 1901)
Vaseline	1879	Robert Cheseborough
Velcro	1948	George de Mestral
Vulcanized rubber	1839	Charles Goodyear
Walkman	1979	Sony
Washing machine, electric	1907	Hurley Machine Co
Waterproof material	1823	Charles Mackintosh
Windmill	644	Persia (Iran)
Wristwatch	1790	Droz and Leschot
Writing	c.3600-3500 BC	Sumerian civilization
X-rays	1895	Wilhelm von Röntgen
Zip fastener	1893	Whitcombe L. Judson

Arts

POETS LAUREATE

In the 15thC Oxford and Cambridge universities gave the title 'laureate' to various poets. The title got its modern status in 1668 when John Dryden was given a stipend to write court poetry and celebrate state occasions in verse.

Name	Appointed	Name	Appointed
Samuel Daniel	1599	Henry James Pye	1790
Ben Jonson	1616	Robert Southey	1813
Sir William d'Avenant	1638	William Wordsworth	1843
John Dryden	1668	Alfred Lord Tennyson	1850
Thomas Shadwell	1689	Alfred Austin	1896
Nathan Tate	1692	Robert Bridges	1913
Nicholas Rowe	1715	John Masefield	1930
Rev. Laurence Eusden	1718	Cecil Day Lewis	1968
Colley Cibber	1730	Sir John Betjeman	1972
William Whitehead	1757	Edward (Ted) Hughes	1984
Thomas Warton	1785	Andrew Motion	1999

BOOKER PRIZE

Established in 1969 by Booker McConnell engineering company for British, Irish and Commonwealth fiction.

Year	Title	Author
1969	*Something to Answer For*	P H Newby
1970	*The Elected Member*	Bernice Rubens
1971	*In a Free State*	V S Naipaul
1972	*G*	John Berger
1973	*The Siege of Krishnapur*	J G Farrell
1974	*The Conservationist*	Nadine Gordimer
	Holiday	Stanley Middleton
1975	*Heat and Dust*	Ruth Prawer Jhabvala
1976	*Saville*	David Storey
1977	*Staying On*	Paul Scott
1978	*The Sea, The Sea*	Iris Murdoch
1979	*Offshore*	Penelope Fitzgerald
1980	*Rites of Passage*	William Golding
1981	*Midnight's Children*	Salman Rushdie
1982	*Schindler's Ark*	Thomas Keneally
1983	*Life and Times of Michael K*	J M Coetzee
1984	*Hotel du Lac*	Anita Brookner
1985	*The Bone People*	Keri Hulme
1986	*The Old Devils*	Kingsley Amis
1987	*Moon Tiger*	Penelope Lively
1988	*Oscar and Lucinda*	Peter Carey
1989	*The Remains of the Day*	Kazuo Ishiguro
1990	*Possession*	A S Byatt
1991	*The Famished Road*	Ben Okri
1992	*Sacred Hunger*	Barry Unsworth
	The English Patient	Michael Ondaatje
1993	*Paddy Clarke Ha Ha Ha*	Roddy Doyle
1994	*How Late It Was, How Late*	James Kelman
1995	*The Ghost Road*	Pat Barker
1996	*Last Orders*	Graham Swift
1997	*The God of Small Things*	Arundhati Roy
1998	*Amsterdam*	Ian McEwan
1999	*Disgrace*	J M Coetzee
2000	*The Blind Assassin*	Margaret Atwood
2001	*True History of the Kelly Gang*	Peter Carey

PULITZER PRIZE

US literature prize established in 1917 by Joseph Pulitzer.

Year	Title	Author
1981	*A Confederacy of Dunces*	John Kennedy Toole
1982	*Rabbit is Rich*	John Updike
1983	*The Color Purple*	Alice Walker
1984	*Ironweed*	William Kennedy
1985	*Foreign Affairs*	Alison Lurie
1986	*Lonesome Dove*	Larry McMurtry
1987	*A Summer to Memphis*	Peter Taylor
1988	*Beloved*	Toni Morrison
1989	*Breathing Lessons*	Anne Tyler
1990	*The Mambo Kings Play Songs of Love*	Oscar Hijelos
1991	*Rabbit at Rest*	John Updike
1992	*A Thousand Acres*	Jane Smiley
1993	*A Good Scent from a Strange Mountain*	Robert Olen Butler
1994	*The Shipping News*	E Annie Proulx
1995	*The Stone Diaries*	Carol Shields
1996	*Independence Day*	Richard Ford
1997	*Angela's Ashes*	Frank McCourt
1998	*American Pastoral*	Philip Roth
1999	*The Hours*	Michael Cunningham
2000	*Interpreter of Maladies*	Jhumpa Lahiri
2001	*The Amazing Adventures of Kavalier and Clay*	Michael Chabon

PRIX GONCOURT

Annual Académie Goncourt prize for a French fiction work.

Year	Title	Author
1981	*Anne-Marie*	Lucien Bodard
1982	*Dans la main de l'ange*	Dominique Fernandez
1983	*Les égarés*	Frederick Tristan
1984	*L'amant*	Marguerite Duras
1985	*Les noces barbares*	Yann Queffelec
1986	*Valet de nuit*	Michel Host
1987	*La nuit sacrée*	Tahir Ben Jelloun
1988	*L'Exposition coloniale*	Erik Orsenna
1989	*Un grand pas vers le Bon Dieu*	Jean Vautrin
1990	*Les champs d'honneur*	Jean Rouault
1991	*Les filles du Calvaire*	Pierre Cambescot
1992	*Texaco*	Patrick Chamoiseau
1993	*Le Rocher de Tanios*	Amin Maalouf
1994	*Un aller simple*	Didier van Cauwelaert
1995	*Le testament français*	Andrei Makine
1996	*Le chasseur Ó*	Pascale Roze
1997	*Le bataille*	Patrick Rambaud
1998	*Confidence pour confidence*	Paul Constant
1999	*Je m'en vais*	Jean Echenoz
2000	*Jean-Jacques Schuhl*	Ingrid Caven Gallimard
2001	*Rouge Brésil*	Jean-Christophe Rufin

NOBEL PRIZE FOR LITERATURE

1901	Rene Sully Prudhomme	1924	Wladyslaw Reymont
1902	Theodor Mommsen	1925	George Bernard Shaw
1903	Bjornestjerne Bjornson	1926	Grazia Deledda
1904	Frederic Mistral/	1927	Henri Bergson
	Juan Echegaray	1928	Sigrid Undset
1905	Henryk Sienkiewicz	1929	Thomas Mann
1906	Giosue Carducci	1930	Sinclair Lewis
1907	Rudyard Kipling	1931	Erik Karlfeldt
1908	Rudolf Eucken	1932	John Galsworthy
1909	Selma Lagerlof	1933	Ivan Bunin
1910	Paul Von Heyse	1934	Luigi Pirandello
1911	Maurice Maeterlinck	1935	*No award*
1912	Gerhart Hauptmann	1936	Eugene O'Neill
1913	Sir Rabindranath Tagore	1937	Roger Martin du Gard
1914	*No award*	1938	Pearl S Buck
1915	Romain Rolland	1939	Frans Eemil Sillanpää
1916	Verner Von Heidenstam	1940-43	*No award*
1917	Karl Gjellerup/Henrik Pontoppidan	1944	Johannes V Jensen
1918	*No award*	1945	Gabriela Mistral
1919	Carl Spitteler	1946	Hermann Hesse
1920	Knut Hamsun	1947	André Gide
1921	Anatole France	1948	Thomas Stearns Eliot
1922	Jacinto Benavente	1949	William Faulkner
1923	William Butler Yeats	1950	Bertrand Russell
		1951	Par Lagerkvist

1952	François Mauriac
1953	Sir Winston Churchill
1954	Ernest Hemingway
1955	Halidor Laxness
1956	Juan Ramón Jiménez
1957	Albert Camus
1958	Boris Pasternak (declined)
1959	Salvatore Quasimodo
1960	Saint-John Perse
1961	Ivo Andric
1962	John Steinbeck
1963	George Seferis
1964	Jean-Paul Sartre (declined)
1965	Mikhail Sholokhov
1966	Shmuel Yosef Agnonnelly Sachs
1967	Miguel Angel Asturias
1968	Yasunan Kawabata
1969	Samuel Beckett
1970	Alexander Solzhenitsyn
1971	Pablo Neruda
1972	Heinrich Böll
1973	Patrick White
1974	Eyvind Johnson/Harry Edmund Martinson
1975	Eugenio Montale
1976	Saul Bellow
1977	V Alexandre
1978	Isaac Bashevis Singer
1979	Odysseus Alepoudhelis
1980	Czeslaw Milosz
1981	Elias Canetti
1982	Gabriel Garcia Márquez
1983	William Gerald Golding
1984	Jaraslav Seifert
1985	Claude Simon
1986	Wole Soyinka
1987	Joseph Brodsky
1988	Naguib Mahfouz
1989	Camilo José Cela
1990	Octavio Paz
1991	Nadine Gordimer
1992	Derek Walcott
1993	Toni Morrison
1994	Kenzaburo Oe
1995	Seamus Heaney
1996	Wislawa Szymborska
1997	Dario Fo
1998	Jose Saramago
1999	Gunther Grass
2000	Gao Xingjian
2001	V.S. Naipaul

THE OSCARS

Year	Best film	Best actor
1927/8	*Wings*	Emil Jannings
1928/9	*Broadway Melody*	Warner Baxter
1929/30	*All Quiet on the Western Front*	George Arliss
1930/1	*Cimarron*	Lionel Barrymore
1931/2	*Grand Hotel*	Frederick March
		Wallace Beery
1932/3	*Cavalcade*	Charles Laughton
1934	*It Happened One Night*	Clark Gable
1935	*Mutiny on the Bounty*	Victor McLaglen
1936	*The Great Ziegfeld*	Paul Muni
1937	*The Life of Emile Zola*	Spencer Tracy
1938	*You Can't Take It With You*	Spencer Tracy
1939	*Gone with the Wind*	Robert Donat
1940	*Rebecca*	James Stewart
1941	*How Green Was My Valley*	Gary Cooper
1942	*Mrs Miniver*	James Cagney
1943	*Casablanca*	Paul Lukas
1944	*Going My Way*	Bing Crosby
1945	*The Lost Weekend*	Ray Milland
1946	*The Best Years of Our Lives*	Fredric March
1947	*Gentleman's Agreement*	Ronald Colman
1948	*Hamlet*	Laurence Olivier
1949	*All the King's Men*	Broderick Crawford
1950	*All About Eve*	José Ferrer
1951	*An American in Paris*	Humphrey Bogart
1952	*The Greatest Show on Earth*	Gary Cooper
1953	*From Here to Eternity*	William Holden

Best actress	Best director
Janet Gaynor	Frank Borzage
Mary Pickford	Frank Lloyd
Norma Shearer	Lewis Milestone
Marie Dressler	Norman Taurog
Helen Hayes	Frank Borzage
Katharine Hepburn	Frank Lloyd
Claudette Colbert	Frank Capra
Bette Davis	John Ford
Luise Rainer	Frank Capra
Luise Rainer	Leo McCarey
Bette Davis	Frank Capra
Vivien Leigh	Victor Fleming
Ginger Rogers	John Ford
Joan Fontaine	John Ford
Greer Garson	William Wyler
Jennifer Jones	Michael Curtiz
Ingrid Bergman	Leo McCarey
Joan Crawford	Billy Wilder
Olivia de Havilland	William Wyler
Loretta Young	Elia Kazan
Jane Wyman	John Huston
Olivia de Havilland	Joseph L Mankiewicz
Judy Holliday	Joseph L Mankiewicz
Vivien Leigh	George Stevens
Shirley Booth	John Ford
Audrey Hepburn	Fred Zinnemann

Year	Best film	Best actor
1954	*On the Waterfront*	Marlon Brando
1955	*Marty*	Ernest Borgnine
1956	*Around the World in Eighty Days*	Yul Brynner
1957	*The Bridge on the River Kwai*	Alec Guinness
1958	*Gigi*	David Niven
1959	*Ben-Hur*	Charlton Heston
1960	*The Apartment*	Burt Lancaster
1961	*West Side Story*	Maximilian Schell
1962	*Lawrence of Arabia*	Gregory Peck
1963	*Tom Jones*	Sidney Poitier
1964	*My Fair Lady*	Rex Harrison
1965	*The Sound of Music*	Lee Marvin
1966	*A Man for All Seasons*	Paul Scofield
1967	*In the Heat of the Night*	Rod Steiger
1968	*Oliver*	Cliff Robertson
1969	*Midnight Cowboy*	John Wayne
1970	*Patton*	George C Scott
1971	*The French Connection*	Gene Hackman
1972	*The Godfather*	Marlon Brando
1973	*The Sting*	Jack Lemmon
1974	*The Godfather Part II*	Art Carney
1975	*One Flew Over the Cuckoo's Nest*	Jack Nicholson
1976	*Rocky*	Peter Finch
1977	*Annie Hall*	Richard Dreyfuss
1978	*The Deer Hunter*	Jon Voight
1979	*Kramer vs Kramer*	Dustin Hoffman
1980	*Ordinary People*	Robert de Niro

Best actress
Grace Kelly
Anna Magnani
Ingrid Bergman

Joanne Woodward
Susan Hayward
Simone Signoret
Elizabeth Taylor
Sophia Loren
Anne Bancroft
Patricia Neal
Julie Andrews
Julie Christie
Elizabeth Taylor
Katharine Hepburn
Katharine Hepburn/
Barbra Streisand
Maggie Smith
Glenda Jackson
Jane Fonda
Liza Minnelli
Glenda Jackson
Ellen Burstyn
Louise Fletcher

Faye Dunaway
Diane Keaton
Jane Fonda
Sally Field
Sissy Spacek

Best director
Elia Kazan
Delbert Mann
George Stevens

David Lean
Vincente Minnelli
William Wyler
Billy Wilder
Robert Wise
David Lean
Tony Richardson
George Cukor
Robert Wise
Fred Zinnemann
Mike Nichols
Carole Reed

John Schlesinger
Franklin J Schaffner
William Friedkin
Bob Fosse
George Roy Hill
Francis Ford Coppola
Milos Forman

John G Avildsen
Woody Allen
Michael Cimino
Robert Benton
Robert Redford

Year	Best film	Best actor
1981	*Chariots of Fire*	Henry Fonda
1982	*Gandhi*	Ben Kingsley
1983	*Terms of Endearment*	Robert Duvall
1984	*Amadeus*	F Murray Abraham
1985	*Out of Africa*	William Hurt
1986	*Platoon*	Paul Newman
1987	*The Last Emperor*	Michael Douglas
1988	*Rain Man*	Dustin Hoffman
1989	*Driving Miss Daisy*	Daniel Day Lewis
1990	*Dances with Wolves*	Jeremy Irons
1991	*Silence of the Lambs*	Anthony Hopkins
1992	*Unforgiven*	Al Pacino
1993	*Schindler's List*	Tom Hanks
1994	*Forest Gump*	Tom Hanks
1995	*Braveheart*	Nicholas Cage
1996	*The English Patient*	Geoffrey Rush
1997	*Titanic*	Jack Nicholson
1998	*Shakespeare in Love*	Roberto Benigni
1999	*American Beauty*	Kevin Spacey
2000	*Gladiator*	Russell Crowe
2001	*A Beautiful Mind*	Denzel Washington

Best actress
Katharine Hepburn
Meryl Streep
Shirley Maclaine
Sally Field
Geraldine Page
Marlee Matlin
Cher
Jodie Foster
Jessica Tandy
Kathy Bates
Jodie Foster
Emma Thompson
Holly Hunter
Jessica Lange
Susan Sarandon
Frances McDormand
Helen Hunt
Gwyneth Paltrow
Hilary Swank
Julia Roberts
Halle Berry

Best director
Warren Beatty
Richard Attenborough
James L Brooks
Milos Forman
Sydney Pollack
Oliver Stone
Bernardo Bertolucci
Barry Levinson
Oliver Stone
Kevin Costner
Jonathan Demme
Clint Eastwood
Steven Spielberg
Robert Zemeckis
Mel Gibson
Anthony Minghella
James Cameron
Stephen Spielberg
Sam Mendes
Steven Soderbergh
Ron Howard

Languages

TYPOGRAPHIC, SCIENTIFIC AND MATHEMATICAL SYMBOLS

+	Addition	−	Subtraction
×	Multiplication	÷	Division
=	Equals	≠	Does not equal
≡	Identical; congruent	≈	Approximately equals
>	Greater than	<	Less than
≫	Much greater than	≪	Much less than
≯	Not greater than	≮	Not less than
≅	Isomorphic	:	Ratio
::	Used between ratios	∞	Infinity
∴	Therefore	∵	Since; because
⇒	Gives; leads on to	∠	Angle
∟	Right angle	⊥	Perpendicular
∇	Nablus	∂	Differential
δ	Delta	λ	Lambda
ε	Epsilon	ν	Nu
μ	Mu	≶	Greater or less than

‖	Parallel	○	Circle
⌒	Arc	△	Triangle
□	Square	▭	Rectangle
▱	Parallelogram	√	Square Root
∑	Sum	∫	Integral
∪	Union	∩	Intersection
∈	Belongs to	⊂	A subset of
{}	Set braces	ø	Empty set absolute value
◁	Normal subgroup of	μ	Mean (population)
σ	Standard deviation (population)	×	Mean (sample)
s	Standard deviation (sample)	π	Ratio of circumference of any circle to its diameter
e	Base of natural logarithms	iff	If and only if
∀	For all	λ	Wavelength
Å	Angstrom unit	μ	Magnetic permeability
Ω	Ohm	h	Planck constant
p	Radius of curvature	&	Ampersand
&c	Etcetera	<	Derived from
{}	Braces	()	Parentheses
[]	Square brackets		

ACCENTS

Name	Character	Example	Name	Character	Example
Acute	´	é	Grave	`	è
Angstrom	°	å	Haček	ˇ	č
Breve	˘	ă	Macron	¯	ā
Cedilla	¸	ç	Tilde	~	ñ
Circumflex	^	î	Umlaut	¨	ü
Diaeresis	¨	ï			

THE APOSTROPHE

One of the most ill-used punctuation marks in the English language.

It is used:

1. To show the possessive case
   a The apostrophe for this should only be used for proper and common nouns and not for the following pronouns: hers, its (it's = it is), ours, theirs, yours.
   b In nouns (sing. and plural) that end in a letter other than *s*, the apostrophe must precede the added *s*, as in the chief's tent, men's boots, the fox's earth.
   c In nouns (sing.) that end in *s*, the possessive is usually formed by adding the 's, as in the octopus's tentacles.
   d In nouns (plural) that end in *s*, the apostrophe must follow the *s*, as in the boys' clothing, the octopuses' tentacles.
   e When the added *s* is silent in speech it is usually omitted, as in for goodness' sake.

f   In English names and surnames add '*s*, as in Burns's poems, St James's Road; but sound often demands the omission of another *s*, as in Bridges' poems.

g   Ancient names ending in s usually omit a further *s*, as in Moses' law, Jesus' love.

h   Abbreviations add '*s* when singular, as in the MP's constituency, and *s*' , when plural, as in MPs' salaries.

2. To show omission
    Examples: e'er (ever), tho' (though), he's (he is, he has), it's (it is), '67 (1967 or contextual century)

don't (do not)	haven't (have not)	shan't (shall not)
shouldn't (should not)	won't (will not)	isn't (is not)
doesn't (does not)	daren't (dare not)	couldn't (could not)
can't (cannot)	mustn't (must not)	hasn't (has not)
there'll (there will)	I'll (I will)	we'll (we will)
you'll (you will)	who'll (who will)	they'll (they will)
I'd (I had, would)	who'd (who would)	I'm (I am)
you're (you are)	who's (who is, *not* pronoun, i.e. whose is that?)	

But note: couldst canst shouldst wouldst

These are the correct grammatical forms, not apostrophe-free abbreviations.

3. Irish names
    Example: O'Reilly.

AMERICAN SPELLING AND WORD VARIATIONS

British	American	British	American
aeroplane	airplane	dialling	dialing
aluminium	aluminum	dialogue	dialog
armoury	armory	draughts (game)	checkers
autumn	fall		
bill	check	dummy (baby)	pacifier
biscuit	cookie	dustbin	garbage can,
braces	suspenders		trashcan
bumbag	fannybag		
calibre	caliber	endeavour	endeavor
callipers	calipers	enfold	infold
callisthenics	calisthenics	enrolled	enroled
car bonnet	hood	epilogue	epilog
car boot	car trunk	estate agent	real-estate
car bumper	fender		agent, realtor
caretaker	janitor		
catalogue	catalog	faeces	feces
centre	center	favour	favor
chemist	druggist,	fervour	fervor
	drugstore	fizzy drink	soda
		flavour	flavor
cheque	check	foetus	fetus
colour	color	gelatine	gelatin
cosy	cozy	glycerine	glycerin
courgette	zucchini	grey	gray
crisps	(potato) chips	grill	broil
cupboard	closet	gynaecology	gynecology
defence	defense	haemorrhage	hemorrhage
demagogue	demagog	harbour	harbor
		honour	honor

British	American	British	American
humour	humor	rateable	ratable
kerb	curb	reconnoitre	reconnoiter
ketchup	catchup	restroom	lavatory
licence	license	return ticket	round-trip ticket
lift	elevator	rigour	rigor
liquorice	licorice	saleable	salable
manoeuvre	maneuver	saloon	sedan
meagre	meager	sanatorium	sanitarium
metre	meter	sceptic	skeptic
motorway	expressway, freeway	single ticket	one-way ticket
		spring onion	scallion
mould	mold	stalls (theatre)	orchestra
nappy	diaper	sulphur	sulfur
neighbour	neighbor	sweets	candies
ochre	ocher	tap	faucet
offence	offense	theatre	theater
off-licence	liquor store	torch	flashlight
organdie	organdy	trainers	sneakers
orthopaedic	orthopedic	tramp	hobo
paediatrics	pediatrics	traveller	traveler
paraffin	kerosene	trousers	pants
pavement	sidewalk	tumour	tumor
pedlar	peddler	underpants	shorts
petrol	gas(oline)	valour	valor
plough	plow	vest	undershirt
postcode	zipcode	waistcoat	vest
pretence	pretense	wallet	billfold
programme	program	whisky	whiskey
pyjamas	pajamas		
railway	railroad		

BRANCHES OF STUDY

Name	Field of Study
Abiology	Inanimate objects
Acarology	Mites, ticks
Actinology	Chemical effects of light in certain wavelengths
Adenology	Glands
Aeroballistics	Science of ballistics as applied to aerodynamics
Aerodynamics	Motions of air and gases, especially in relation to moving objects
Aerography	Atmospheric conditions
Aerolithology	Meteors
Aerolitics	Aerolites (stormy meteors)
Aerology	Planet Mars
Aerometry	Properties of air
Aeronautics	Technology of flying aeroplanes
Aerophysics	Earth's atmosphere (especially effects of high-speed flying bodies)
Aerostatics	Construction/operation of lighter-than- air craft such as balloons
Aesthetics	Principles of beauty and the beautiful
Aetiology	Philosophy of causation
Agmatology	Bone fractures
Agriology	Comparative study of the customs of primitive peoples
Agrobiology	Soil management
Agrogeology	Adaptability of land to agriculture
Agrology	Crop production
Agronomy	Management in farming
Agrostology	Grasses (*also called* graminology)
Alethiology	Branch of logic concerned with truth and error

Name	Field of Study
Algebra	Branch of mathematics which uses letters and other symbols to represent numbers, values, etc.
Algology	Seaweeds and algae
Alimentology	Nutrition (*also called* trophology)
Allergology	Allergies
Ambrology	Sources/formation of amber
Ampelography	Grapes
Amphibiology	Amphibians
Anatomy	Human body and its parts
Anemology	Winds
Angiology	Blood vessels and lymphatic system
Anthoecology	Flowers and their environment
Anthropometry	Proportions, size and weight of human body
Anthropogeny	Human origins
Anthropogeography	Geographical distribution of mankind and its relationship with the environment
Anthropography	Geographical distribution of different races
Anthropology	Mankind, especially origins and customs
Anthroposociology	Sociology of race using anthropological methods
Antinology	Chemical effects of light in certain wavelengths
Apiology	Honey bees
Apologetics	Defences or proofs of Christianity
Arachnology	Spiders
Archaeogeology	Geological features of distant past
Archaeology	Human remains and artefacts
Architectonics	(1) Systematization of knowledge
	(2) Science of architecture
Archology	(1) Science of origins
	(2) Science of government
Areology	Planet Mars
Aretaics	Study of virtue

Name	Field of Study
Arthrology	Joints of the body
Assyriology	Ancient Assyria
Astrogation	Space navigation
Astrogeology	Geological features of celestial bodies, especially the moon and solar planets
Astrognosy	Fixed stars
Astrolithology	Meteorites (*also called* meteoritics)
Astronautics	Space travel
Astronomy	Celestial bodies
Astrophysics	Origins and physical nature of celestial bodies
Atmology	Water vapour
Audiology	Hearing (especially impaired)
Autecology	Ecology of an individual plant or species
Autoecology	Relation of organisms to their environment
Avigation	Aerial navigation
Avionics	Electrical/electronic equipment used in aviation
Axiology	Values (ethics, aesthetics, religion, etc.)
Azoology	Inanimate nature
Bacteriology	Bacteria
Ballistics	Projectiles and firearms
Batology	Brambles
Bibliography	History of books
Bibliology	Doctrines of Bible
Bibliotics	Analysis of handwriting, especially manuscripts
Bioastronautics	Effects of space travel, especially on human body
Biochemistry	Chemical processes in living organisms
Bioclimatology	Relationship between living creatures and atmospheric conditions
Biodynamics	Physiological processes of plants and animals
Bioecology	Interrelationship of plant and animal life in a shared environment

Name	Field of Study
Biogeography	Geographical distribution of plants and animals
Biolinguistics	Relationship between physiology and speech
Biology	All living organisms
Bionics	How living creatures perform tasks and how this knowledge can be applied to automated or computer-driven equipment
Bionomics	*See* ecology
Biophysiology	Growth, structure and physiology of organs
Biostatics	Relationship between structure and function of plants and animals
Biotechnology	*See* ergonomics
Botany	All plant life (*also called* phytology)
Bryology	Mosses and liverworts
Cacogenics	Factors that influence degeneration in offspring, especially with respect to different races
Cambistry	Commercial exchange, especially international money values
Cardioangiology	Heart and blood vessels
Cardiodynamics	Forces and movements of the heart
Cardiology	Heart and its functions
Caricology	Sedges
Carpology	Fruits and seeds
Cartography	Map-making
Casuistry	Relationship of general ethical principles to particular problems
Catoptrics	Light reflection
Cecidiology	Galls produced on trees by fungi, etc.
Cetology	Whales
Chemistry	Composition, properties and behaviour of substances
Chondrology	Cartilage

Name	Field of Study
Chorology	Migrations and distributions of organisms
Chrematistics	Wealth
Christology	Nature and attitudes of Christ
Chromatology	Colours
Chrysology	Production of wealth, especially related to precious metals
Cinematography	Art of making cinema films
Climatology	Climates
Cliometrics	Application of mathematical principles to the study of history
Coccidology	Coccidea family (scales, mealy bugs, etc.)
Codicology	Early manuscripts
Coleopterology	Beetles, weevils
Conchology	Mollusc shells (*also called* malacology)
Cosmology	(1) Overall structure of physical universe (astronomy) (2) Origin, structure and evolution of universe (philosophy)
Criminology	Crime and criminals
Crustaceology	Crustaceans
Crustalogy	Surface of earth or moon
Cryogenics	Low temperatures and their effects
Cryology	Snow, ice
Cryptography	Secret writing, codes
Ctetology	Origin and development of acquired characteristics
Cultural anthropology	Creative achievements of societies
Cybernetics	Comparative study of complex electronic machines and human nervous system
Cynology	Dogs
Cytochemistry	Chemistry of living cells

Name	Field of Study
Cytology	Cells
Cytotechnology	Human cells, especially to detect cancer
Dactylography	Fingerprints
Dactylology	Sign language using hands
Demography	Vital and social statistics of populations
Demology	Human activities and social environments
Demonology	Demons
Dendrochronology	Examination of annual growth rings in trees to determine age
Dendrology	Trees
Deontology	Ethics
Dermatology	Skin, skin diseases
Desmidiology	Microscopic, unicellular algae
Desmopathology	Diseases of ligaments and tendons
Diabology	The Devil
Diagnostics	Diagnosis of illness/diseases
Didactics	Art/science of teaching
Dioptrics	Light refraction
Diplomatology	Analysis of original texts or documents
Dipterology	Diptera family (flies, mosquitoes, gnats, etc.)
Ecclesiology	Church building and decoration
Eccrinology	Secretions and secretory glands
Echinology	Sea urchins
Ecology	Relationship of living organisms to their environment (*also called* bionomics)
Economics	Production and distribution of wealth
Egyptology	Ancient Egypt
Electrobiology	Electrical activity in organisms/effect of electricity on organisms
Emblematology	Interpretation of emblems
Emetology	Causes of vomiting

Name	Field of Study
Emmenology	Menstruation
Endocrinology	Endocrine glands
Enterology	Intestines
Entomology	Insects (*also called* insectology)
Enzymology	Fermentation and enzymes (*also called* zymology)
Epidemiology	Incidence, distribution, control and prevention of diseases
Epigraphy	Deciphering and interpreting ancient inscriptions
Epiphytology	Plant diseases
Epistemology	Human knowledge, especially methods and validity of
Epizoology	Incidence and spread of animal diseases
Eremology	Deserts
Ergology	Physical and mental effects of work
Ergonomics	Relationship of man to his working environment (*also called* biotechnology)
Eschatology	Death and final destiny
Ethics	Moral principles and right action
Ethnology	Origin and development of all races and their relationships with each other
Ethology	Animal behaviour in relation to the environment
Etiology	Causes of diseases and why they spread
Etruscology	Etruscan civilization
Etymology	Origin and history of words
Eugenics	Improvement of a breed or species through selective breeding
Euthenics	Improvement of a race or breed by controlling external influences such as environment
Exegetics	Interpretation of biblical literature
Exobiology	Life beyond earth's atmosphere
Faunology	*See* zoogeography

Name	Field of Study
Filicology	Ferns (*also called* pteridology)
Fluviology	Watercourses, rivers
Foetology	Foetuses
Fromology	Cheese
Gastrology	Stomach functions and diseases
Gemmology	Gemstones
Genecology	Animal species and their environments
Genesiology	Human reproduction
Genetics	Heredity
Geodynamics	Forces within the earth
Geognosy	Constituent parts of the earth
Geogony	Formation of the earth
Geology	The earth
Geometry	Properties and relationships of angles, points, lines, surfaces and solids
Geomorphology	Earth's surface
Geratology	Ageing
Geriatrics	Care of the aged
Gerodontics	Dental problems of the aged
Glaciology	Glaciers
Glottogony	Origin of language
Glottology	Science of linguistics
Gnoseology	Philosophy of knowledge
Graminology	*See* agrostology
Grammar	Formal structure of a language
Graphology	Analysis of handwriting
Gynaecology	Disorders of the female reproductive system
Gyniatrics	Women's diseases
Gyrostatics	Rotating solid bodies
Haematology	Blood, diseases of the blood and blood-forming tissues

Name	Field of Study
Hagiography	Lives of the saints
Halology	Salts
Hamartiology	Doctrine of sin
Helcology	Ulcers
Helminthology	Worms (especially internal worms)
Hemipterology	Hemiptera family (bedbugs, aphids, etc.)
Heparology, hepatology	The liver
Heraldry	Genealogy (especially aristocratic lineage)
Hermeneutics	Interpretation and explanation (especially interpretation of the Bible)
Herniology	Hernias
Herpetology	Reptiles and amphibians
Heterology	Abnormalities of tissue structure
Hippiatrics	Horse diseases (*also called* hippopathology)
Hippology	Horses
Hippopathology	*See* hippiatrics
Histology	Microscopic features of animal and plant tissues
History	Past events, especially human affairs
Horometry	Measuring time
Horticulture	Cultivation of gardens
Hydraulics	Engineering applications of laws applying to water and other liquids in motion
Hydrodynamics	Forces acting on or produced by liquids (*also called* hydromechanics)
Hydrogeology	Water on/below the earth's surface
Hydrokinetics	Laws of gases/liquids in motion
Hydrology	Water on the earth and in the atmosphere
Hydromechanics	*See* hydrodynamics
Hydroponics	Growing plants in special solutions instead of soil
Hydrostatics	Equilibrium and pressure of liquids

Name	Field of Study
Hyetography	Geographical distribution of rainfall
Hygienics	Health and hygiene
Hygrology	Atmospheric humidity
Hymenopterology	Hymenoptera family (bees, wasps, ants, etc.)
Hypnology	Sleep, hypnotism
Hypsography	Land areas above sea level
Hysterology	The uterus
Iamatology	Remedies
Iatrochemistry	Application of chemistry for healing purposes
Ichnology	Fossil footprints
Ichthyology	Fish
Immunogenetics	Immunity with respect to genetic formation
Immunology	Immunity from disease
Insectology	*See* entomology
Isagogics	Biblical writings, emphasizing the literature and cultural history of the Bible
Kinematics	Motion of objects without reference to the external forces which cause the motion
Kinesics	'Body language' or non-verbal gestures of communication (*also called* pasimology)
Kinetics	Motion of objects with reference to the external forces acting on them
Koniology	Atmospheric dust and other airborne pollutants
Lalopathology	Speech disorders
Laryngology	Larynx
Lepidopterology	Butterflies and moths
Lexicology	The form, development and meaning of words
Lichenology	Lichens
Limnology	Ponds, lakes
Linguistics	Language and its structure
Lithology	Mineral composition and structure of rocks

Name	Field of Study
Liturgiology	Church rituals and their symbolism
Logistics	Movement and supply of troops
Macrobiotics	Longevity
Malacology	*See* conchology
Mammalogy	Mammals
Mathematics	Abstract study of number, quantity and space
Mensuration	Science of measurement
Merology	Body fluids and basic tissues
Metaethics	Foundation of ethics
Metalinguistics	Language in its cultural context
Metallurgy	Science of producing, refining and use of metals
Metamathematics	Logical analysis of basic principles of mathematics
Metaphysics	Theoretical study of being and knowing
Meteoritics	*See* astrolithology
Meteorology	Climate and weather variations
Methodology	(1) Application of reason to science and philosophy
	(2) The science of method (order) and classification
Metoposcopy	*See* physiognomy
Metrology	Science of weights and measures
Miasmology	Fogs, smogs
Microbiology	Micro-organisms
Micrology	Microscopic objects
Mineralogy	Minerals (*also called* oryctology)
Momiology	Mummies
Morphology	(1) Form and structure of animals and plants
	(2) Word formation patterns
Morphonomy	Laws of form in nature
Muscology	Mosses
Mycology	Fungi
Myology	Muscles, musculature
Myrmecology	Ants

Name	Field of Study
Nealogy	Early stages of animal development
Neonatology	The newborn
Neontology	Recently living plants and animals
Neossology	Young birds
Nephology	Clouds
Nephrology	Kidneys
Neurology	Nerves and nerve systems (especially diseases of)
Neuropsychiatry	Diseases of the mind and nervous system
Neuropterology	Neuroptera family (lacewings, etc.)
Nidology	Birds' nests
Noology	Intuition and reason
Obstetrics	Care of women before, during and after childbirth
Oceanography	Oceans, seas
Odontology	Teeth and surrounding tissues
Oenology	Making wines (*also called* viticulture)
Olfactology	Scientific study of the sense of smell
Ombrology	Rainfall
Oncology	Tumours
Oneirology	Science and interpretation of dreams
Onomastics	Names and their origins
Oology	Birds' eggs
Ophiology	Snakes
Ophthalmology	Eyes, eye diseases and defects
Optics	Properties of light (*also called* photology)
Organology	Organs of plants and animals
Ornithology	Birds
Orology	Scientific study of mountains
Orthodontics	Malformed teeth and other oral problems
Orthoepy	Correct pronunciation
Orthography	Correct spelling
Orthology	Correct use of language

Name	Field of Study
Orthopaedics	Bone and muscle deformities
Orthopsychiatry	Prevention of mental/behavioural disorders
Orthopterology	Orthoptera family (cockroaches, grasshoppers, etc.)
Orthoptics	Eye irregularities, especially muscle problems
Oryctology	*See* mineralogy
Osmonosology	Disorders of the sense of smell
Osteology	Bones and diseases of
Otolaryngology	Ear, nose and throat
Otology	Diseases of the ear
Ovology	Formation and structure of animal ova
Paedeutics	Science of learning
Paediatrics	Medical care of infants, children and adolescents
Paedogogics	Science or art of teaching/education
Palaeobiology	Fossil plants and animals
Palaeobotany	Fossil plants
Palaeoecology	Plants, animals and their environment in the distant past
Palaeoethnology	Early man
Palaeogeography	Features of the earth as they existed in past geological ages
Palaeography	Ancient writings
Palaeoichthyology	Fossil fish
Palaeology	Antiquities
Palaeomammalogy	Mammals of past ages
Palaeontology	Life in the geological past
Palaeopedology	Soils of past geological ages
Palaeopathology	Diseases from the distant past
Palaeornithology	Fossil birds
Palaeozoology	Fossil animals
Pantology	Systematic survey of all branches of learning
Parapsychology	Psychic phenomena

Name	Field of Study
Paroemiology	Proverbs
Pasimology	*See* kinesics
Pathognomy	The emotions and signs or expressions of emotion
Pathology	Causes, origin and nature of disease
Pedodontics	Children's dental care
Pedology	(1) Soils
	(2) Physical and psychological events of childhood
Pelycology	Pelvic structure
Penology	(1) Science of the punishment of crime
	(2) Science of the management of prisons
Perastadics	Space flying
Periodontics	Diseases of bone, tissue and gum (mouth)
Petrogenesis	Formation of rocks
Petrology	Origin, structure and composition of rocks
Phaenology	Climate and its effects on living organisms
Pharmacology	Preparation, use, effects and dosage of drugs
Pharyngology	Pharynx
Phenology	Organisms as affected by climate (e.g. migration of birds, blooming of flowers)
Philology	Science of language
Philosophy	Enquiry into truths and knowledge of reality
Phletology	Veins of the body
Phonetics	Vocal sounds (and their classification)
Phorology	Disease carriers, epidemics and endemic diseases
Photics	Light
Photodynamics	Light in relation to the movement of plants
Photology	*See* optics
Phyllotaxy	Arrangement and distribution of leaves
Physics	Interactions of matter and energy
Physiognomy	Determining aspects of character from physical, especially facial, features (*also called* metoposcopy)

Name	Field of Study
Physiography	Physical geography
Physiology	Functions of organisms and their parts
Phytobiology	Plant biology
Phytogeography	Geographical distribution of plants
Phytology	*See* botany
Pistology	Characteristics of faith
Pneumology	Human respiratory system
Polemics	History of ecclesiastical disputes
Pomology	Fruit
Ponerology	Sin, evil and wrong-doing
Potamology	Rivers
Praxeology	Human behaviour and conduct
Proctology	Disorders of rectum and anus
Protozoology	Protozoa (minute invertebrates, e.g. amoeba)
Psephology	Elections
Psychiatry	Study, treatment and prevention of mental illness
Psychodiagnostics	Evaluation of personality
Psycholinguistics	Relationship between language and behaviour patterns
Psychology	The mind and mental processes, emotions and desires
Psychopathology	Causes and nature of mental illness
Psychopharmacology	Drugs that alter emotional and mental conditions
Psychotherapy	Treating psychological disorders using psychological methods
Pteridology	*See* filicology
Pyretology	Fevers
Pyrology	Fire and heat, especially chemical analysis of
Radiogenetics	Effects of radioactivity on genes
Radiology	Radiation for diagnosis and therapy
Rhinology	The nose and its diseases

Name	Field of Study
Robotics	Application of automated machinery to accomplish tasks normally done by hand
Seismography	Measurement of earthquakes
Selenology	Moon
Semantics	Meaning of words (*also called* semasiology, sematology, semology)
Semiotics	Signs
Semitics	Semitic languages and culture
Serology	Serums
Siagonology	Jaw bones
Sindology	Funeral shrouds
Sinology	Chinese culture
Sociology	Origin, development, structure and function of human society
Somatology	Man's physical characteristics
Sophiology	Science of ideas
Speleology	Caves
Sphagnology	Sphagnum mosses
Sphygmology	The pulse
Splanchnology	Viscera (large internal organs of the body)
Spongology	Sponges
Statics	Matter and forces at rest or in equilibrium
Stirpiculture	Selective breeding
Stomatology	Diseases of the mouth
Stratigraphy	Stratified rocks
Sumerology	Sumerian civilization
Syndesmology	Ligaments of the body
Synecology	Relationships of various groups of organisms to a common environment
Syntax	Principles of grammatical sentence construction
Taxonomy	Principles of classification

Name	Field of Study
Tectonics	The earth's crust
Teleology	Ends or final causes with particular reference to evidence of purpose or design in nature
Telmatology	Wetlands, marshes, swamps
Tenology	Tendons
Teratology	Malfunctions in animals and plants
Testaceology	Shell-bearing animals
Thalassography	Areas of water such as gulfs, sounds, etc.
Thanatology	Death and the dead
Thaumatology	Miracles
Theology	Theistic religions (especially Christianity)
Theoretics	Theories and hypotheses (applied to any field of learning)
Thermodynamics	Relationship between heat and other types of energy
Thermogeography	Geographical factors affecting temperature
Thermokinematics	Movement of heat
Thermostatics	Equilibrium of heat
Thremmatology	Breeding of domestic plants and animals
Topology	(1) Characteristics of geometrical figures that remain unaffected by changes in shape or size (2) Plant localities
Toponymy	Place-names of a district
Toxicology	Poisons
Traumatology	Wounds and their treatment
Trichology	Hair and hair diseases
Trigonometry	Relationships of sides and angles of triangles
Trophology	*See* alimentology
Typhlology	Blindness and its prevention
Uranography	Studying and mapping the heavens
Urbanology	Urban problems and conditions

Name	Field of Study
Uredinology	Branch of mycology which studies rusts
Urology	Diseases of the kidney
Venereology	Venereal diseases
Vexillology	Flags, flag design
Virology	Viruses
Viticulture	*See* oenology
Volcanology	Volcanoes
Xylology	Structure of wood
Zenography	Jupiter (planet)
Zoobiology	*See* zoology
Zoogeography	Geographical distribution of animal life (also called faunology)
Zoology	All living creatures (*also called* zoobiology)
Zoopathology	Animal diseases
Zoophysiology	Animal physiology
Zoophytology	Zoophytes (animals such as sponges, corals, etc.)
Zoopsychology	Animal behaviour
Zymology	*See* enzymology

PHOBIAS

A phobia is defined as an intense dislike or irrational fear of a given situation or thing. Phobia is Greek for 'fear'; Phobos was a Greek god who inspired fear and terror in his enemies.

Fear of	Phobia
accidents	dystychiphobia
ageing	gerascophobia
air sickness	aeronausiphobia
air (fresh), draughts	aerophobia (*see also* flying)
alcohol	methyphobia
alcohol (drinking)	dipsophobia
amnesia	amnesiophobia
animals	zoophobia
animals (wild)	agrizoophobia
animal skin, fur	doraphobia
ants	myrmecophobia
atomic energy	nucleomitophobia
attack	scelerophobia
auroral lights	auroraphobia
bacteria	bacillophobia
baldness	peladophobia
bathing	bathophobia (*see also* depth)
beards	pogonophobia
beaten (being)	rhabdophobia (*see also* magic)
bed (going to)	clinophobia
bees	apiphobia
bicycles	cyclophobia
birds	ornithophobia

Fear of	Phobia
blood	hemaphobia
blushing	erythrophobia (*see also* red)
body odour	bromhidrosiphobia
books	bibliophobia
bound (being)	merinthophobia
bridges (crossing)	gephyrophobia
buildings (high)	batophobia
bulls	taurophobia
buried alive (being)	taphephobia
cancer	carcinomophobia
cats	ailurophobia
Celts, Celtic	Celtophobia
cemeteries	coimetrophobia
certain places	topophobia (*see also* performing)
changes (making)	tropophobia
childbirth	tocophobia
China, Chinese	Sinophobia
choking	pnigophobia
cholera	cholerophobia
clothes	vestiophobia
clouds	nephophobia
cold	cheimaphobia
colours	chromophobia
comets	cometophobia
complex scientific (or Greek) terms	Hellenologophobia
computers	computerphobia
constipation	coprostasophobia
corpses, death	necrophobia
crossing streets	agiophobia

Fear of	Phobia
crowded rooms	koinoniphobia
crowds	demophobia
crucifixes	staurophobia
dampness	hygrophobia
dancing	chorophobia
darkness	nyctophobia
dawn	eosophobia
daylight	phengophobia
death, corpses	necrophobia
decaying matter	septophobia
decisions	decidophobia
defecation (painful)	defecalgesiophobia
deformity	dysmorphophobia
demons, goblins	bogyphobia
dentists	dentophobia
depth	bathophobia (*see also* bathing)
devils, evil spirits	demonophobia
diabetes	diabetophobia
dining, dinner conversation	deipnophobia
dirt	mysophobia
dirt (on oneself)	automysophobia
disease	nosophobia
disease (hereditary)	patriophobia
disease, illness	pathophobia
disease (particular)	monopathophobia
disease (rectal)	proctophobia
disease (skin)	dermatosiophobia
dizziness	dinophobia
doctors	iatrophobia
dogs	cynophobia

Fear of	Phobia
dolls	pedophobia
double vision	diplopiaphobia
draughts, fresh air	aerophobia (*see also* flying)
draughts, winds	anemophobia
dreams	oneirophobia
dreams (wet)	oneirogmophobia
drink (usually alcohol)	potophobia
drugs	pharmacophobia
drugs (new)	neopharmaphobia
dryness	xerophobia
dust	amathophobia
duty (neglect of)	paralipophobia
electricity	electrophobia
emetics, vomiting	emetophobia
empty rooms	kenophobia
enclosed spaces	clithrophobia
England, English	Anglophobia
everything	panophobia
evil spirits, devils	demonophobia
excrement	coprophobia
eyes	ommatophobia
eyes (opening one's)	optophobia
fabrics (particular)	textophobia
failure	kakorrhaphiophobia
fat (becoming)	obesophobia
fatigue	kopophobia
fear	phobophobia
feathers	pteronophobia
fever	pyrexiphobia
filth	rhypophobia

Fear of	Phobia
fire	pyrophobia
fish	ichthyophobia
flashes of light	selaphobia
flavours	geumophobia
flowers	anthophobia
flying	aerophobia (*see also* air (fresh), draughts)
fog	homichlophobia
food	cibophobia
foreigners	xenophobia
France, French	Francophobia
freedom	eleutherophobia
fresh air, draughts	aerophobia (*see also* flying)
frogs, toads	batrachophobia
frost, ice	cryophobia
fur, animal skin	doraphobia
gaiety	cherophobia
garlic	alliumphobia
genitals (female)	eurotophobia
Germany, Germans	Germanophobia
ghosts	phasmophobia
girls (young)	parthenophobia
glass	crystallophobia
goblins, demons	bogyphobia
God	theophobia
gold	aurophobia
gravity	barophobia
Greek (or complex scientific) terms	Hellenologophobia
hair	chaetophobia
hair disease	trichinophobia

Fear of	Phobia
heart attack	angionophobia
heart disease	cardiophobia
heat	thermophobia
heavens	uranophobia
heights	acrophobia
hell	hadephobia
high buildings	batophobia
high places (looking up at)	anablepophobia
home	domatophobia
home (returning to)	nostophobia
homosexuals	homophobia
horses	hippophobia
hospitals	nosocomephobia
hurricanes	lilapsophobia
ice, frost	cryophobia
ideas	ideophobia
illness, disease	pathophobia
immobility (of a joint)	ankylophobia
imperfection	atelophobia
infection	molysomophobia
infinity	apeirophobia
injections	trypanophobia
injury (physical)	traumatophobia (*see also* war)
insanity	lyssophobia (*see also* madness)
insects	entomophobia
insect stings	cnidophobia
Japan, Japanese	Japanophobia
jealousy	zelophobia
Jews, Judaism	Judaeophobia

Fear of	Phobia
jumping (from both high and low places)	catapedaphobia
justice	dikephobia
kissing	philemaphobia
knees	genuphobia
lakes	limnophobia
large objects	megalophobia
laughter	gelophobia
learning	sophophobia
left hand side of the body (objects on)	levophobia
leprosy	lepraphobia
lice	pediculophobia
light	photophobia
light (flashes of)	selaphobia
lightning	astraphobia
lights (glaring)	photaugiophobia
locked in (being)	claustrophobia
long waits	macrophobia
looked at (being)	scopophobia
love	philophobia
lying, myths and stories	mythophobia
machinery	mechanophobia
madness	maniaphobia (*see also* insanity)
magic	rhabdophobia (*see also* beaten, being)
making changes	tropophobia
marriage	gamophobia
materialism	hylephobia (*see also* woods)
meat	carnophobia
memories	mnemophobia

Fear of	Phobia
men	androphobia
meningitis	meningitophobia
menstruation	menophobia
metal	metallophobia
meteors	meteorophobia
mice	musophobia
microbes	microbiophobia
mind	psychophobia
mirrors	catoptrophobia
missiles	ballistophobia
mites, ticks	acarophobia
money (touching)	chrematophobia
monsters (or giving birth to a monster)	teratophobia
moon	selenophobia
mother-in-law	pentheraphobia
motion	kinesophobia
motor vehicles	motorphobia
music	musicophobia
myths, stories and lying	mythophobia
name (a particular name or word)	onomatophobia
narrowness	anginaphobia
needles	enetophobia
needles, pins	belonephobia
Negroes	negrophobia
night	noctiphobia
noise	acoustiphobia
nosebleeds	epistaxiophobia
novelty	cainophobia

Fear of	Phobia
nudity	gymnophobia
objects (large)	megalophobia
objects (pointed)	aichmophobia
objects (sacred)	hierophobia
objects (small)	tapinophobia
open spaces	agoraphobia
opinions (others')	allodoxaphobia
opposite sex	sexophobia
outer space	spacephobia
pain	algophobia
paper	papyrophobia
parasites	parasitophobia
parents-in-law	soceraphobia
penis (contour of, visible through clothes)	medectophobia
penis (erect)	ithyphallophobia
people	anthropophobia
performing (stagefright)	topophobia (*see also* places (certain))
philosophy, philosophers	philosophobia
physical injury	traumatophobia (*see also* war)
pins, needles	belonephobia
places (certain)	topophobia (*see also* performing)
places (steep)	cremnophobia
plants	botanophobia
pleasure	hedonophobia
pointed obects	aichmophobia
poisoned (being)	toxiphobia
poisons	iophobia (*see also* rust)
politicians	politicophobia
pope	papaphobia

Fear of	Phobia
poverty	peniaphobia
progress	prosophobia
prostitutes	cyprianophobia
pseudo-rabies	kynophobia (*see also* rabies)
punishment	poinephobia
purple	porphyrophobia
rabies	hydrophobia (*see also* pseudo-rabies)
radiation, X-rays	radiophobia
railways	siderodromophobia
rain	ombrophobia
red	erythrophobia (*see also* blushing)
relatives	syngenesophobia
religious ceremonies	teletophobia
reptiles	herpetophobia
responsibility	hypengyophobia
ridicule	katagelophobia
riding in vehicles	amaxophobia
right-hand side of the body (objects on)	dextrophobia
rivers	potamophobia
robbers	harpaxophobia
rooms (empty)	kenophobia
rooms (crowded)	koinoniphobia
ruin	atephobia
Russia, Russian	Russophobia
rust	iophobia (*see also* poisons)
sacred objects	hierophobia
saints	hagiophobia
Satan	Satanophobia
school	didaskaleinophobia

Fear of	Phobia
scientific terms (complex) or Greek terms	Hellenologophobia
scratched (being)	amychophobia
sea	thalassophobia
semen	spermatophobia
sex, opposite	sexophobia
sexual abuse	agraphobia
sexual feelings	erotophobia
sexual intercourse	coitophobia
shadows	sciophobia
shellfish	ostraconophobia
shock	hormephobia
sin	hamartophobia
single, staying	anuptaphobia
sitting down	thaasophobia
sitting still	cathisophobia
skin	dermatophobia
skin disease	dermatosiophobia
Slavs, Slavic	Slavophobia
sleep	hypnophobia
slime	blennophobia
small objects	tapinophobia
smells	olfactophobia
snakes	ophidiophobia
snow	chionophobia
solitude	autophobia
sourness	acerophobia
space (outer)	spacephobia
spaces (enclosed)	clithrophobia
spaces (open)	agoraphobia

Fear of	**Phobia**
speaking aloud	phonophobia
spectres	spectrophobia
speed	tachophobia
spiders	arachnophobia
stage fright	topophobia (*see also* places (certain))
stairs	climacophobia
standing	stasiphobia
standing and walking	stasibasiphobia
stars	siderophobia
staying single	anuptaphobia
stories, myths and lying	mythophobia
streets (crossing)	agiophobia
stuttering	psellismophobia
sunlight	heliophobia
surgery	tomophobia
swallowing	phagophobia
symbols	symbolophobia
syphilis	syphiliphobia
taking tests	testophobia
talking	laliophobia
tapeworms	taeniophobia
technology	technophobia
teeth	odontophobia
teleology	teleophobia
telephones	telephonophobia
termites	isopterophobia
tests, taking	testophobia
tetanus (lockjaw)	tetanophobia
theatres	theatrophobia

Fear of	Phobia
theology	theologicophobia
thieves	kleptophobia
thinking	phronemophobia
thirteen	triskaidekaphobia
thunder	brontophobia
thunder and lightning	keraunophobia
ticks, mites	acarophobia
time	chronophobia
toads, frogs	batrachophobia
tombstones	placophobia
touching, being touched	aphephobia
touching money	chrematophobia
travel	hodophobia
trembling	tremophobia
tuberculosis	phthisiophobia
tyrants	tyrannophobia
undressing (in front of someone)	dishabillophobia
untidiness	ataxiophobia
urinating	urophobia
vaccination, vaccines	vaccinophobia
vegetables	lachanophobia
vehicles, riding in	amaxophobia
venereal disease	cypridophobia
vertigo	illyngophobia
virginity, losing one's	primeisodophobia
vomiting, emetics	emetophobia
walking	basiphobia
walking and standing	stasibasiphobia
war	traumatophobia (*see also* injury (physical))

Fear of	Phobia
washing oneself	ablutophobia
wasting sickness	tabophobia
water	hydrophobia
waves (sea)	cymophobia
weakness	asthenophobia
wet dreams	oneirogmophobia
white	leukophobia
wine	oenophobia
women	gynaephobia
women (beautiful)	venustaphobia
woods	hylephobia (*see also* materialism)
word (a particular word or name)	onomatophobia
words	logophobia
work	ergasiophobia
worms	scoleciphobia
wrinkles (getting)	rhytiphobia
writing	graphophobia
wrongdoing	peccatiphobia
X-rays, radiation	radiophobia
young girls	parthenophobia

COLLECTIVE NOUNS

Noun	Collective term	Noun	Collective term
actors	company	flowers	bouquet
aldermen	bench, guzzle	geese	flock, gaggle or skein
antelopes	herd		
apes	shrewdness	giraffes	herd
bakers	tabernacle	gnats	swarm or cloud
bears	sleuth	goats	herd or tribe
bees	swarm or grist	goldfinches	charm
birds	flock, flight or congregation	grouse	brood, covey or pack
bishops	bench	gulls	colony
buffaloes	herd	hares	down or husk
bullfinches	bellowing	hens	flock
cattle	herd or drove	herons	sedge or siege
chickens	brood	herrings	shoal or glean
cranes	herd, sedge or siege	horses	herd or drove
critics	shrivel	hounds	pack, mute or cry
crocodiles	bask	insects	swarm
cubs	litter	inventions	budget
curlews	herd	jellyfish	stuck, smuth
deer	herd	judges	bench
directors	board	kangaroos	troop
doves	flight or dule	larks	exaltation
ducks	team or padding	leopards	leap
eggs	clutch	lions	pride or troop
fish	catch	magpies	tiding
fish	shoal or run	mares	stud
flies	swarm or grist	monkeys	troop

Noun	Collective term	Noun	Collective term
oxen	yoke, drove, team or herd	rumours	nest
		sailors	crew
partridges	covey	seals	herd, pod or rookery
people	audience, crowd, congregation or mob	sheep	flock
		ships	fleet
pigeons	flock or flight	sparrows	host
pigs	litter	stories	anthology
plovers	stand or wing	swallows	flight
policemen	posse	swans	herd or bevy
ponies	herd	swifts	flock
porpoises	school or gam	swine	herd, sounder or dryft
poultry	run		
prisoners	gang	thieves	gang
pups	litter	whales	pod
quails	bevy	wolves	pack, rout or herd
quotation	mellificium, rosary	workmen	gang
rabbits	nest		
racehorses	string or field		
ravens	unkindness		
remedies	rabble		
rooks	building or clamour		

-ARCHIES AND -OCRACIES

The suffixes -archy and -ocracy mean 'government by'.
Therefore, in the following list hierocracy means
'government by priests' and triarchy means
'government by three people'.

Anarchy	Without law
Aristocracy	Privileged order
Autocracy	One man absolute rule
Bureaucracy	Officials
Democracy	The people
Despotocracy	A tyrant
Diarchy	Two rulers
Ergatocracy	The workers
Ethnocracy	Race or ethnic group
Gerontocracy	Old men
Gynarchy	Women
Gynaecocracy	Women
Gynocracy	Women
Hierocracy	Priests
Isocracy	All with equal power
Kakistocracy	The worst
Matriarchy	A mother (or mothers)
Meritocracy	In power on ability
Mobocracy	A mob
Monarchy	Hereditary head of state
Monocracy	One person
Ochlocracy	The mob
Oligarchy	Small exclusive class

Pantisocracy	All with equal power
Patriarchy	Male head of family
Plutocracy	The wealthy
Stratocracy	The military
Technocracy	Technical experts
Thearchy	God or gods
Theocracy	Divine guidance
Triarchy	Three people

Sport

OLYMPIC GAMES VENUES

I	1896	Athens, Greece
II	1900	Paris, France
III	1904	St Louis, USA
IV	1908	London, UK
V	1912	Stockholm, Sweden
VI		Allocated to Berlin (*not held*)
VII	1920	Antwerp, Belgium
VIII	1924	Paris, France
IX	1928	Amsterdam, The Netherlands
X	1932	Los Angeles, USA
XI	1936	Berlin, Germany
XII		Allocated to Tokyo, then Helsinki (*not held*)
XIII		Allocated to London (*not held*)
XIV	1948	London, UK
XV	1952	Helsinki, Finland
XVI	1956	Melbourne, Australia
XVII	1960	Rome, Italy
XVIII	1964	Tokyo, Japan
XIX	1968	Mexico City, Mexico
XX	1972	Munich, FRG
XXI	1976	Montreal, Canada
XXII	1980	Moscow, USSR
XXIII	1984	Los Angeles, USA
XXIV	1988	Seoul, South Korea
XXV	1992	Barcelona, Spain
XXVI	1996	Atlanta, USA
XXVII	2000	Sydney, Australia
XXVIII	2004	Athens, Greece

WINTER OLYMPIC GAMES VENUES

I	1924	Chamonix, France
II	1928	St Moritz, Switzerland
III	1932	Lake Placid, USA
IV	1936	Garmisch-Partenkirchen, Germany
	1940	Games allocated to Sapporo, then St Moritz, then Garmisch-Partenkirchen (*not held*)
	1944	Games allocated to Cortina (*not held*)
V	1948	St Moritz, Switzerland
VI	1952	Oslo, Norway
VII	1956	Cortina, Italy
VIII	1960	Squaw Valley, USA
IX	1964	Innsbruck, Austria
X	1968	Grenoble, France
XI	1972	Sapporo, Japan
XII	1976	Innsbruck, Austria
XIII	1980	Lake Placid, USA
XIV	1984	Sarajevo, Yugoslavia
XV	1988	Calgary, Canada
XVI	1992	Albertville, France
XVII	1994	Lillehammer, Norway*
XVIII	1998	Nagano, Japan
XIX	2002	Salt Lake City, USA

The two-year gap between Winter Olympics was introduced so that in the future there will be an Olympic games every two years, rather than both Winter and Summer Olympics occurring in the same year every four years.

1996 ATLANTA OLYMPIC GAMES FINAL MEDAL TABLES

There were 271 competitions in total.

Country	Gold	Silver	Bronze	Total
United States	44	32	25	101
Germany	20	18	27	65
Russia	26	21	16	63
China	16	22	12	50
Australia	9	9	23	41
France	15	7	15	37
Italy	13	10	12	35
South Korea	7	15	5	27
Cuba	9	8	8	25
Ukraine	9	2	12	23
Canada	3	11	8	22
Hungary	7	4	10	21
Romania	4	7	9	20
Netherlands	4	5	10	19
Poland	7	5	5	17
Spain	5	6	6	17
Bulgaria	3	7	5	15
Brazil	3	3	9	15
Britain	1	8	6	15
Belarus	1	6	8	15
Japan	3	6	5	14
Czech Republic	4	3	4	11
Kazakstan	3	4	4	11
Greece	4	4	0	8

Country	Gold	Silver	Bronze	Total
Sweden	2	4	2	8
Kenya	1	4	3	8
Switzerland	4	3	0	7
Norway	2	2	3	7
Denmark	4	1	1	6
Turkey	4	1	1	6
New Zealand	3	2	1	6
Belgium	2	2	2	6
Nigeria	2	1	3	6
Jamaica	1	3	2	6
South Africa	3	1	1	5
North Korea	2	1	2	5
Ireland	3	0	1	4
Finland	1	2	1	4
Indonesia	1	1	2	4
Yugoslavia	1	1	2	4
Algeria	2	0	1	3
Ethiopia	2	0	1	3
Iran	1	1	1	3
Slovakia	1	1	1	3
Argentina	0	2	1	3
Austria	0	1	2	3
Armenia	1	1	0	2
Croatia	1	1	0	2
Portugal	1	0	1	2
Thailand	1	0	1	2
Namibia	0	2	0	2
Slovenia	0	2	0	2

Country	Gold	Silver	Bronze	Total
Malaysia	0	1	1	2
Moldova	0	1	1	2
Uzbekistan	0	1	1	2
Georgia	0	0	2	2
Morocco	0	0	2	2
Trinidad & Tobago	0	0	2	2
Burundi	1	0	0	1
Costa Rica	1	0	0	1
Ecuador	1	0	0	1
Hong Kong	1	0	0	1
Syria	1	0	0	1
Azerbaijan	0	1	0	1
Bahamas	0	1	0	1
Latvia	0	1	0	1
Philippines	0	1	0	1
Taiwan	0	1	0	1
Tonga	0	1	0	1
Zambia	0	1	0	1
India	0	0	1	1
Israel	0	0	1	1
Lithuania	0	0	1	1
Mexico	0	0	1	1
Mongolia	0	0	1	1
Mozambique	0	0	1	1
Puerto Rico	0	0	1	1
Tunisia	0	0	1	1
Uganda	0	0	1	1

COMMONWEALTH GAMES VENUES

The title has changed four times.

British Empire Games
I	1930	Hamilton, Canada
II	1934	London, England
III	1938	Sydney, Australia
IV	1950	Auckland, New Zealand

British Empire and Commonwealth Games
V	1954	Vancouver, Canada
VI	1958	Cardiff, Wales
VII	1962	Perth, Australia
VIII	1966	Kingston, Jamaica

British Commonwealth Games
IX	1970	Edinburgh, Scotland
X	1974	Christchurch, New Zealand

Commonwealth Games
XI	1978	Edmonton, Canada
XII	1982	Brisbane, Australia
XIII	1986	Edinburgh, Scotland
XIV	1990	Auckland, New Zealand
XV	1994	Victoria, Canada
XVI	1998	Kuala Lumpur, Malaysia
XVII	2002	Manchester, England

FOOTBALL WORLD CUP VENUES

1930	Uruguay	1962	Chile	1986	Mexico
1934	Italy	1966	England	1990	Italy
1938	France	1970	Mexico	1994	USA
1950	Brazil	1974	W Germany	1998	France
1954	Switzerland	1978	Argentina	2002	S Korea/Japan
1958	Sweden	1982	Spain		

FOOTBALL

	FA Cup	Scottish FA Cup	Football League Cup
1990	Manchester United	Aberdeen	Nottingham Forest
1991	Tottenham Hotspur	Motherwell	Sheffield Wednesday
1992	Liverpool	Rangers	Manchester United
1993	Arsenal	Rangers	Arsenal
1994	Manchester United	Dundee United	Aston Villa
1995	Everton	Celtic	Liverpool
1996	Manchester United	Rangers	Aston Villa
1997	Chelsea	Kilmarnock	Leicester City
1998	Arsenal	Hearts	Chelsea
1999	Manchester United	Rangers	Tottenham Hotspur

	Scottish League Cup	Football League	Scottish League
1990	Aberdeen	Liverpool	Rangers
1991	Rangers	Arsenal	Rangers
1992	Hibernian	Leeds United	Rangers
1993	Rangers	Manchester United	Rangers
1994	Rangers	Manchester United	Rangers

	Scottish League Cup	Football League	Scottish League
1995	Raith Rovers	Blackburn Rovers	Rangers
1996	Aberdeen	Manchester United	Rangers
1997	Rangers	Manchester United	Rangers
1998	Celtic	Arsenal	Celtic
1999	Rangers	Manchester United	Rangers

	European Cup	Cup Winners' Cup	UEFA Cup
1990	AC Milan	Sampdoria	Juventus
1991	Red Star Belgrade	Manchester United	Inter Milan
1992	Barcelona	Werder Bremen	Ajax Amsterdam
1993	Marseille	AC Parma	Juventus
1994	AC Milan	Arsenal	Inter Milan
1995	Ajax Amsterdam	Real Zaragoza	Parma
1996	Juventus	Paris St Germain	Bayern Munich
1997	Borussia Dortmund	FC Barcelona	FC Schalke
1998	Real Madrid	Chelsea	Inter Milan
1999	Manchester United	Lazio	Parma

	World Cup		Olympics
1974	W Germany	1976	GDR
1978	Argentina	1980	Czechoslovakia
1982	Italy	1984	France
1986	Argentina	1988	USSR
1990	W Germany	1992	Spain
1994	Brazil	1996	Nigeria
1998	France		

CRICKET

	County Champions	Nat West Trophy
1990	Middlesex	Lancashire
1991	Essex	Hampshire
1992	Essex	Northamptonshire
1993	Middlesex	Warwickshire
1994	Warwickshire	Worcestershire
1995	Warwickshire	Warwickshire
1996	Leicestershire	Lancashire
1997	Glamorgan	Essex
1998	Leicestershire	Lancashire
1999	Surrey	Gloucestershire

RUGBY UNION

	International	CIS Insurance County	Allied Dunbar English
1990	Scotland	Lancashire	Wasps
1991	England	Cornwall	Bath
1992	England	Lancashire	Bath
1993	France	Lancashire	Bath
1994	Wales	Yorkshire	Bath
1995	England	Warwickshire	Leicester
1996	England	Gloucestershire	Bath
1997	France	Cumbria	Wasps
1998	France	Chesire	Newcastle Falcons
1999	Scotland	Cornwall	Leicester

	SWALEC Welsh	Tennents Premier	Tetley's Bitter
1990	Neath	Melrose	Bath
1991	Llanelli	Boroughmuir	Harlequins
1992	Llanelli	Melrose	Bath
1993	Llanelli	Melrose	Leicester
1994	Cardiff	Melrose	Bath
1995	Swansea	Stirling County	Bath
1996	Pontypridd	Melrose	Bath
1997	Cardiff	Melrose	Leicester
1998	Llanelli	Watsonians	Saracens
1999	Swansea	Heriot's	Wasps

	Tennents Velvet	Heineken European Champions Cup
1996	Hawick	–
1997	Melrose	Brive (France)
1998	Glasgow Hawks	Bath
1999	Gala	Ulster

RUGBY LEAGUE

	Premiership	Challenge Cup	JJB Super League
1990	Wigan	Wigan	–
1991	Wigan	Wigan	–
1992	Wigan	Wigan	–
1993	Wigan	Wigan	–
1994	Wigan	Wigan	–
1995	Wigan	Wigan	–
1996	Wigan	St Helens	St Helens
1997	Bradford	Bradford Bulls	St Helens
1998	–	Wigan	Sheffield
1999	–	St Helens	Leeds

GOLF

	Open	World Matchplay	PGA
1990	N Faldo (GB)	I Woosnam (GB)	M Harwood (Aus)
1991	I Baker-Finch (Aus)	S Ballesteros (Spa)	S Ballesteros (Spa)
1992	N Faldo (GB)	N Faldo (GB)	T Johnstone (Zim)
1993	G Norman (Aus)	C Pavin (US)	B Langer (Ger)
1994	N Price (Zim)	E Els (S Afr)	J M Olazabal (Spa)
1995	J Daly (US)	E Els (S Afr)	B Langer (Ger)
1996	T Lehman (US)	E Els (S Afr)	C Rocca (Ita)
1997	J Leonard (US)	E Els (S Afr)	I Woosnam (GB)
1998	M O'Meara (US)	M O'Meara (US)	C Montomerie (Sco)
1999	P Lawrie (GB)	J Maggert (US)	C Montomerie (Sco)

	US Open	US Masters	US PGA
1990	H Irwin (US)	N Faldo (GB)	W Grady (Aus)
1991	P Stewart (US)	I Woosnam (GB)	J Daly (US)
1992	T Kite (US)	F Couples (US)	N Price (Zim)
1993	L Janzen (US)	B Langer (Ger)	P Azinger (US)
1994	E Els (SA)	J M Olazábal (Spa)	N Price (US)
1995	C Pavin (US)	Ben Crenshaw (US)	S Elkington (Aus)
1996	S Jones (US)	N Faldo (GB)	M Brooks (US)
1997	E Els (S Afr)	T Woods (US)	D Love (US)
1998	L Janzen (US)	M O'Meara (US)	V Singh (Fiji)
1999	P Stewart (US)	J M Olazábal (Spa)	T Woods
2000		V Singh (Fiji)	

	Ryder Cup	Walker Cup	Curtis Cup
1990			US
1991	US	US	
1992			GB & Ireland
1993	US	US	
1994			GB & Ireland
1995	Europe	GB & Ireland	
1996			GB & Ireland
1997	Europe	US	
1998			US
1999	US	GB & Ireland	

TENNIS

Wimbledon

	Men's Singles	Women's Singles
1990	S Edberg (Swe)	M Navratilova (US)
1991	M Stich (Ger)	S Graf (Ger)
1992	A Agassi (US)	S Graf (Ger)
1993	P Sampras (US)	S Graf (Ger)
1994	P Sampras (US)	C Martinez (Spa)
1995	P Sampras (US)	S Graf (Ger)
1996	R Krajicek (Neth)	S Graf (Ger)
1997	P Sampras (US)	M Hingis (Swi)
1998	P Sampras (US)	J Novotna (Czech Rep)
1999	P Sampras (US)	L Davenport (US)

US Open

	Men's Singles	Women's Singles
1990	P Sampras (US)	G Sabatini (Arg)
1991	S Edberg (Swe)	M Seles (Yug)
1992	S Edberg (Swe)	M Seles (Yug)
1993	P Sampras (US)	S Graf (Ger)
1994	A Agassi (US)	A Sanchez-Vicario (Spa)
1995	P Sampras (US)	S Graf (Ger)
1996	P Sampras (US)	S Graf (Ger)
1997	P Rafter (Aus)	M Hingis (Swi)
1998	P Korda (Czech Rep)	M Hingis (Swi)
1999	A Agassi (US)	S Williams (US)

French Open

Men's Singles	Women's Singles
1990 A Gomez (Ecu)	M Seles (Yug)
1991 J Courier (US)	M Seles (Yug)
1992 J Courier (US)	M Seles (Yug)
1993 S Bruguera (Spa)	S Graf (Ger)
1994 S Bruguera (Spa)	A Sanchez-Vicario (Spa)
1995 T Muster (Aut)	S Graf (Ger)
1996 Y Kafelnikov (Rus)	S Graf (Ger)
1997 G Kuerten (Bra)	I Majoli (Cro)
1998 C Moya (Spa)	A Sanchez-Vicario (Spa)
1999 A Agassi (US)	S Graf (Ger)

Australian Open

Men's Singles	Women's Singles
1990 I Lendl (Cz)	S Graf (FRG)
1991 B Becker (Ger)	M Seles (Yug)
1992 J Courier (US)	M Seles (Yug)
1993 J Courier (US)	M Seles (Yug)
1994 P Sampras (US)	S Graf (Ger)
1995 A Agassi (US)	M Pierce (Fr)
1996 B Becker (Ger)	M Seles (US)
1997 P Sampras (US)	M Hingis (Swi)
1998 P Korda (Czech Rep)	M Hingis (Swi)
1999 Y Kafelnikov (Rus)	M Hingis (Swi)
2000 A Agassi (US)	L Davenport (US)

HORSE RACING

	Grand National	Cheltenham Gold Cup	1000 Guineas
1990	Mr Frisk	Norton's Coin	Salsabil
1991	Seagram	Garrison Savannah	Shadayid
1992	Party Politics	Cool Ground	Hatoof
1993	declared void	Jodami	Sayyedati
1994	Miinnehoma	The Fellow	Las Meninas
1995	Royal Athlete	Master Oats	Harayir
1996	Rough Quest	Imperial Call	Bosra Sham
1997	Lord Gyllene	Mr Mulligan	Sleepytime
1998	Earth Summit	Cool Dawn	Cape Verdi
1999	Bobbyjo	See More Business	Wince
2000	Papillon	Looks Like Trouble	Lahan

	2000 Guineas	Oaks	Derby
1990	Tirol	Salsabil	Quest for Fame
1991	Mystiko	Jet Ski Lady	Generous
1992	Rodrigo de Triano	User Friendly	Dr Devious
1993	Zafonic	Intrepidity	Commander in Chief
1994	Mister Baileys	Balanchine	Erhaab
1995	Pennekamp	Moonshell	Lammtarra
1996	Mark of Esteem	Lady Carla	Shaamit
1997	Entrepreneur	Reams of Verse	Benny the Dip
1998	King of Kings	Shatoush	High Rise
1999	Island Sands	Ramruma	Oath
2000	King's Best		

	Ascot Gold Cup	St Leger	King George VI & Queen Elizabeth Diamond Stakes
1990	Ashal	Snurge	Belmoz
1991	Indian Queen	Toulon	Generous
1992	Drum Taps	User Friendly	St Jovite
1993	Drum Taps	Bob's Return	Opera House
1994	Arcadian Heights	Moonax	King's Theatre
1995	Double Trigger	Classic Cliché	Lammatarra
1996	Classic Cliché	Shantou	Pentire
1997	Celeric	Silver Patriarch	Swain
1998	Kayf Tara	Nedawi	Swain
1999	Enzeili	Mutafaweq	Daylami

General Interest

INTERNATIONAL TIME ZONES

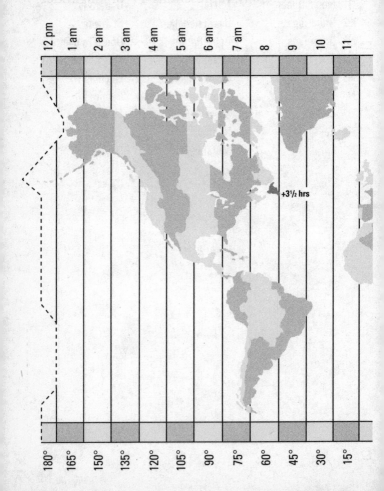

The system was established in 1884 by agreement between the major countries. The meridian of longitude passing through Greenwich Observatory, London, was taken as the starting-point for 24 time zones (each, generally, representing 15° of longitude,

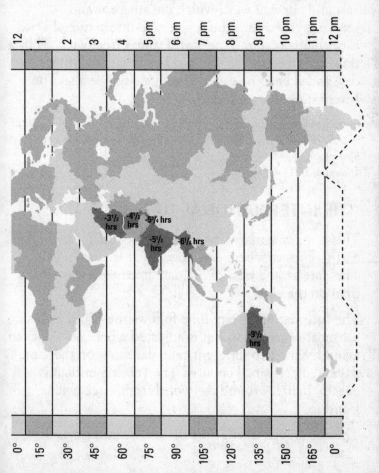

the equivalent of 1 hour). There are 12 time zones west of Greenwich and 12 east. Within a time zone the time is the same throughout, but when crossing from one zone to another, the time changes by 1 hour. The world is divided into 23 full zones and 2 half zones, zone 12 east and zone 12 west, which are adjacent and separated by an imaginary line, the International Date Line, halfway round the world from Greenwich. Thus a traveller crossing the line and heading west will lose a day, and if heading east will gain a day. See also **The International Date Line.**

Note: Several countries, including the UK, use Daylight Saving Time (DST) in order to maximize daylight time in summer. Clocks are put forward 1 hour in spring and back 1 hour in autumn. The above plan does not take account of DST adjustments.

THE INTERNATIONAL DATE LINE

This is an imaginary line which marks the place on the earth's surface where each new calendar day begins. The date on the west of the date line is one day later than on the east.

The International Date Line follows the 180th meridian for most of its length but is adjusted where necessary to avoid having two different calendar dates on the same day in a fairly small country. The 180th meridian is exactly halfway round the world from Greenwich, London.

The sun travels over 15° of the earth's surface each

hour. For each 15° west of Greenwich, the time reverses one hour. At longitude 180° east the time is 12 hours ahead of Greenwich time. At longitude 180° west, the time is 12 hours behind Greenwich. Thus there is a 24-hour time difference between the two sides of the 180th meridian.

A new date begins first on the western side of the date line. As the earth rotates on its axis, this new date sweeps westwards over the earth and the date covers the entire earth in 24 hours. See also **International Time Zones**.

CALENDARS

There are three main types of calendar:

Lunar Calendar
Most ancient calendars used the interval between successive full moons, the lunar month, as a measure of time. The lunar month is approximately 29½ days in length; thus a lunar year (12 x 29½) amounts to approximately 354 days. This means that its year is approximately 11 days shorter than the true solar year (approximately 365 days), and following it would cause the seasons to occur earlier and earlier each year. This makes the lunar calendar alone unsuitable for practical use.

Solar Calendar
The solar calendar adheres as closely as possible to the length of the solar year, but assumes a set length of month, thereby

disregarding the lunar month. The solar year is 365.2422 days in length. Solar calendars use a normal year of 365 days and allow for the fraction (0.2422 days) by inserting an extra day every fourth year. The solar calendar has 4 critical points: 2 equinoxes and 2 solstices (see page 234). The fact that the equinoxes always occur on or about the same days each year establishes the accuracy of such a calendar.

Lunisolar Calendar

The lunisolar calendar is an attempt to reconcile the differences between the lunar and solar calendars. The lunar month of 29½ days becomes either a 29- or 30-day month (alternately), thus making 354 days. Additional months are inserted from time to time to adjust the number of calendar days to the number of days in a solar year. This is usually done by inserting a 13th lunar month every 2 or 3 years, thus ensuring that the seasons accord approximately with the calendar period.

CALENDARS IN USE TODAY

Gregorian Calendar

The Gregorian calendar is used almost universally throughout the western world, and has been used in Great Britain since 1752. It was calculated by Pope Gregory XIII in the 1580s in an attempt to reform the Roman Julian calendar which had become inaccurate and confusing. As the true length of the solar year was then known, Gregory simplified and adapted the Julian calendar accordingly.

The Gregorian calendar has 12 months, 11 with either 30 or 31 days; February has 28 days and, every fourth year (a leap year), 29 days. However, these adjustments are still not quite enough to ensure absolute accuracy and so in century years that cannot be divided by 400 (1700, 1800, 1900), February loses its leap year. The Gregorian calendar is so accurate that the difference between calendar and solar years is approximately 26 seconds. This difference will increase by 0.53 second each century because the solar year is gradually becoming shorter. The western calendar is based on the year of Jesus Christ's birth; dates before this event are noted BC (Before Christ), and those after, as AD (Anno Domini, In the Year of our Lord). Non-Christians often prefer BCE (Before Christian Era) and CE (Christian Era).

Month	Derived from	Length (days)
January	*Januarius* (Latin). The Roman god, Janus, faces two ways and was often represented on doorways and archways.	31
February	*Februarius* (Latin). Taken from Februa, a purification rite which took place on February 15.	28 or 29
March	*Martius* (Latin). Mars was the Roman god of war.	31
April	*Aprilis* (Latin). Taken from aperire ('to open'), referring to the trees and flowers which are beginning to open.	30
May	*Maius* (Latin). Derived either from Maia, a Roman goddess identified with the Greek goddess Maia, or from *maiores* ('elders'), referring to the period in which old people were honoured.	31

Month	Derived from	Length (days)
June	*Junius* (Latin). Derived either from the goddess Juno or *iuniores* ('young people'), indicating the period which was traditionally dedicated to young people.	30
July	*Julius* (Latin). Named after Gaius Julius Caesar, the Roman soldier and statesman.	31
August	*Augustus* (Latin). Named after Augustus Caesar, the first Roman Emperor.	31
September	*Septem* (Latin), meaning 'seven'; September was originally the seventh month in the Roman calendar.	30
October	*Octo* (Latin), meaning 'eight'; October was originally the eighth month in the Roman calendar.	31
November	*Novem* (Latin), meaning 'nine'; November was originally the ninth month in the Roman calendar.	30
December	*Decem* (Latin), meaning 'ten'; December was originally the tenth month in the Roman calendar.	31

The Christian Church Calendar is governed partly by the sun and partly by the moon. The dates of fixed feasts such as Christmas and saints' days relate to the solar calendar, whereas the date of Easter – and therefore of all the movable feasts and holy days – is determined by the date of the Paschal Full Moon.

Jewish Calendar

The Jewish calendar was begun, traditionally, at the moment of creation, 3,760 years and 3 months before the beginning of the Christian era. To find the Jewish year, add 3,760 years to the date in the Gregorian calendar. Thus, the Gregorian year 2000 will be 5760 in the Jewish calendar. As a lunisolar calendar, the Jewish calendar requires an extra month (Veadar) to be inserted seven times in a 19-year cycle; Veadar is inserted between Adar and Nisan and Adar is given 30 days instead of 29.

Month	Length (days)
Nisan	(March/April in Gregorian calendar) 30
Iyar	29
Sivan	30
Tammuz	29
Ab	30
Elul	29
Tishri	30
Heshvan	29/30
Kislev	29/30
Tebet	29
Shebat	30
Adar	29/30

Note: Nisan is the first month of the Jewish year, although years are numbered from Tishri, the seventh month.

Islamic Calendar

The Islamic calendar begins with Muhammad's flight from Mecca to Medina (the Hegira) in AD 622. As a lunar calendar the year is much shorter than the solar year and, as no adjustments are made, it moves fully backwards through the seasons over a period of 32½ years. Time is divided into 30-year cycles; during each cycle 19 years have the usual 354 days and 11 years take an extra day each. The Islamic year is based on the moon and has 12 months, alternately of 30 and 29 days.

Month	Length (days)
Muharram	30
Safar	29
Rabi I	30
Rabi II	29
Jumada I	30
Jumada II	29
Rajab	30
Shaban	29
Ramadan	30
Shawwal	29
Zulkadah	30
Zulhijjah	29*

Takes an extra day in leap years.

Hindu Calendar
The Hindu calendar dates from about 1000 BC and was first used in India. It is a lunar calendar, so an additional month (Adhik) is incorporated every 30 months to remove the discrepancy between the lunar year (approximately 354 days) and the solar year (approximately 365 days). There are 12 months of 30 days each, divided into Shukla (the light fortnight) and Krishna (the dark fortnight).

Hindu Month Names

Chait'r (March/April in Gregorian calendar)	Vaishaakh
Jayshyth	Aashaadh
Shraawan	Bhaadrap'd
Aashwin	Kaartik
Maargasheersh	Paush
Maagh	Phaalgun

Chinese Calendar

The Chinese calendar began in 2637 BC when Emperor Huangdi is said to have invented it. It is a lunar calendar and years are calculated in cycles of 60 (e.g. 2000 is the 17th year in the 78th cycle).

There is a Buddhist belief that the Buddha invited all the animals to celebrate the New Year with him but only 12 came. As a reward the Buddha named a year after each of them in the order in which they arrived in his presence, with the rat first and the pig last.

The Chinese year is based on the moon and has 12 months, each beginning at a new moon with 29 or 30 days. A month is repeated seven times during each 19-year cycle so that the calendar stays approximately in line with the seasons. The Chinese New Year occurs at the second new moon after the beginning of winter; thus it is no earlier than 20 January and no later than 20 February.

Note: The official Chinese calendar now corresponds with the western system, but the old calendar is still used in Tibet, Hong Kong, Singapore, Malaysia and other parts of south-east Asia.

Animal	Year								
Rat	1900	1912	1924	1936	1948	1960	1972	1984	1996
Buffalo or Cow	1901	1913	1925	1937	1949	1961	1973	1985	1997
Tiger	1902	1914	1926	1938	1950	1962	1974	1986	1998
Rabbit	1903	1915	1927	1939	1951	1963	1975	1987	1999
Dragon	1904	1916	1928	1940	1952	1964	1976	1988	2000
Snake	1905	1917	1929	1941	1953	1965	1977	1989	2001
Horse	1906*	1918	1930	1942	1954	1966*	1978	1990	2002
Goat	1907	1919	1931	1943	1955	1967	1979	1991	2003
Monkey	1908	1920	1932	1944	1956	1968	1980	1992	2004
Rooster or Chicken	1909	1921	1933	1945	1957	1969	1981	1993	2005
Dog	1910	1922	1934	1946	1958	1970	1982	1994	2006
Pig	1911	1923	1935	1947	1959	1971	1983	1995	2007

Called Fire Horse once every 60 years

FRENCH REVOLUTIONARY CALENDAR

The French Revolutionary Calendar was an attempt by the First French Republic to reform the Gregorian calendar in line with revolutionary principles. It was adopted in 1793 and abandoned in 1805.

Vendémiaire (Month of Grape Harvest)	23 September–22 October
Brumaire (Month of Mist)	23 October–21 November
Frimaire (Frosty Month)	22 November–21 December
Nivôse (Snowy Month)	22 December–20 January
Pluviôse (Rainy Month)	21 January–19 February
Ventôse (Windy Month)	20 February–21 March
Germinal (Month of Buds)	22 March–20 April
Floréal (Month of Flowers)	21 April–20 May
Prairial (Month of Meadows)	21 May–19 June
Messidor (Month of Harvest)	20 June–19 July
Thermidor (Month of Heat)	20 July–18 August
Fructidor (Month of Fruit)	19 August–22 September

SOLSTICE

The time when the sun is farthest from the equator and appears to stand still. Occurs twice yearly:

Winter Solstice (around 22 December) = shortest day
Summer Solstice (around 21 June) = longest day

EQUINOX

The time when the sun crosses the equator and day and night are equal. Occurs twice yearly:

Spring (Vernal) Equinox (around 21 March)
Autumnal Equinox (around 23 September)

QUARTER DAYS (ENGLAND, WALES AND NORTHERN IRELAND)

The four days of the year when certain payments become due.

Lady Day	25 March
Midsummer	24 June
Michaelmas	29 September
Christmas	25 December

SCOTTISH TERM DAYS

A division of the academic year when schools, colleges or universities are in session, and one of the periods of time during which sessions of courts of law are held.

Candlemas 2 February	Feast of the Purification of the Virgin Mary and the day on which church candles are blessed.
Whit Sunday 7th Sunday after Easter	Commemorates the descent of the Holy Spirit after Easter (movable) on the day of Pentecost. Whit (or white) Sunday was so called because white robes were worn on that day.
Lammas 1 August	Feast commemorating St Peter's miraculous delivery from prison. Formerly observed in England as a Harvest Festival, when loaves made from the first ripe corn were consecrated. (Origin: Old English *hlafmaesse*, 'loaf mass'.)
Martinmas 11 November	Feast of St Martin, formerly day for hiring servants and slaughtering cattle to be salted for the winter.

BIRTHSTONES, ASTROLOGICAL SIGNS AND NAMES

Month	Gem	Characteristic
January	Garnet	Constancy
February	Amethyst	Sincerity
March	Aquamarine, Bloodstone	Courage
April	Diamond	Innocence
May	Emerald	Love
June	Pearl, Alexandrite, Moonstone	Health
July	Ruby	Contentment
August	Peridot, Sardonyx	Married happiness
September	Sapphire	Clear thinking
October	Opal, Tourmaline	Hope
November	Topaz	Faithfulness
December	Turquoise, Zircon	Wealth

Corresponding Astrological (Zodiac) Sign*

Aquarius (20 January–18 February)

Pisces (19 February–20 March)

Aries (21 March–19 April)

Taurus (20 April–20 May)

Gemini (21 May–20 June)

Cancer (21 June–22 July)

Leo (23 July–22 August)

Virgo (23 August–22 September)

Libra (23 September–22 October)

Scorpio (23 October–21 November)

Sagittarius (22 November–21 December)

Capricorn (22 December–19 January)

Astrological signs do not correspond exactly with the beginning and end of the month; birthdate should be the guide to the appropriate gemstone.

WEDDING ANNIVERSARIES

Year	Gift
1	Paper, plastics, furniture
2	Cotton, china
3	Leather or artificial leather articles
4	Linen, silk or synthetic silks
5	Wood and decorative articles for the home
6	Iron
7	Wood, copper, brass
8	Bronze, electrical appliances
9	Pottery, china, glass, crystal
10	Tin, aluminium
11	Steel
12	Linen, silk, nylon
13	Lace
14	Ivory, agate
15	Crystal, glass
20	China, small items of furniture
25	Silver
30	Pearls or personal gifts
35	Coral, jade
40	Rubies, garnets
45	Sapphires, tourmalines,
50	Gold
55	Emeralds, turquoises
60, 75	Diamonds, gold

ORDERS OF PRECEDENCE

The Peerage

Title Royal Duke/Duchess
Style His Royal Highness the Duke of . . . /
Her Royal Highness the Duchess of . . .
Addressed as Sir or, formally, May it please your Royal Highness

Title Archbishop
Style The Most Reverend His Grace the Lord Archbishop of . . .
Addressed as My Lord Archbishop or Your Grace

Title Duke/Duchess
Style His Grace the Duke of . . . /
Her Grace the Duchess of . . .
Addressed as My Lord Duke/
Your Grace; Dear Madam/Duchess*

Title Marquess/Marchioness
Style The Most Honourable the Marquess of . . . /
The Most Honourable the Marchioness of . . .
Addressed as My Lord/My Lord; Madam/Lady*

Title Earl/Countess
Style The Right Honourable The Earl of . . . /
The Right Honourable the Countess of . . .
Addressed as My Lord/My Lord; Madam/Madam*

Title Viscount/Viscountess
Style The Right Honourable the Viscount . . . /
The Right Honourable the Viscountess . . .
Addressed as My Lord/My Lady; Madam/Lady*

Title Bishop
Style The Right Reverend the Lord Bishop of . . .
Addressed as My Lord

Title Baron/Baroness
Style The Right Honourable the Lord . . . /
The Right Honourable the Lady . . .
Addressed as My Lord/Lord; My Lady/Lady*

* This section shows the correct forms of address for letters (formal) and when speaking (formal)

ORDERS OF CHIVALRY

Title The Most Noble Order of the Garter
Date 1348
Abbrev. KG
Ribbon Garter blue
Motto Honi soit qui mal y pense (Shame on him who thinks evil of it)
Limit 24

Title The Most Ancient and Most Noble Order of the Thistle
Date Revived 1687
Abbrev. KT

Ribbon Green
Motto Nemo me impune lacessit (No one provokes me with impunity)
Limit 16

Title The Most Honourable Order of the Bath
Date 1725
Abbrev. GCB, KCB, DCB, CB
Ribbon Crimson
Motto Tria juncta in uno (Three joined in one)

Title The Order of Merit
Date 1902
Abbrev. OM
Ribbon Blue and crimson
Limit 24

Title The Most Exalted Order of the Star of India
Date 1861
Abbrev. GCSI, KCSI, CSI
Ribbon Light blue with white edges
Motto Heaven's light our guide

Note: No conferments have been made since 1947.

Title The Most Distinguished Order of St Michael and St George
Date 1818
Abbrev. GCMG, KCMG, DCMG, CMG
Ribbon Saxe blue with scarlet centre
Motto Auspicum melioris aevi (Token of a better age)

Title The Most Eminent Order of the Indian Empire
Date 1868
Abbrev. GCIE, KCIE, CIE
Ribbon Imperial purple
Motto Imperatricis auspiciis (Under the auspices of the Empress)

Note: No conferments have been made since 1947.

Title The Distinguished Service Order
Date 1886
Abbrev. DSO
Ribbon Red with blue edges

Title The Imperial Service Order
Date 1902
Abbrev. ISO
Ribbon Crimson with blue centre

Title The Royal Victorian Chain
Date 1902

Title The Imperial Order of the Crown of India (for ladies only)
Date 1877
Abbrev. CI
Badge Royal cipher surmounted by heraldic crown with bow of
light blue watered ribbon, edged white

Note: No conferments have been made since 1947.

Title The Royal Victorian Order
Date 1896
Abbrev. GCVO, KCVO, DCVO, CVO, LVO, MVO
Ribbon Blue, with white and red edges
Motto Victoria

Title The Most Excellent Order of the British Empire
Date 1917
Abbrev. GVE, DBE, CBE, OBE, MBE
Ribbon Rose pink edged with light grey; military division has vertical grey stripe in centre, civil division does not
Motto For God and the Empire

Title The Order of the Companions of Honour
Date 1917
Abbrev. CH
Ribbon Carmine with gold edges
Limit 65

Baronetage and Knightage
Title Baronet
Style 'Sir' before forename and surname, followed by 'Bt'
Wife 'Lady' followed by surname

Title Knight
Style 'Sir' before forename and surname, followed by 'Bt' (if applicable), plus appropriate initials (KGC, KC, etc.)
Wife 'Lady' plus surname

PRINCIPAL BRITISH ORDERS AND DECORATIONS IN ORDER OF PRECEDENCE

Title	Date of Institution	Abbreviation
Knight of the Garter	1348	KG
Knight of the Thistle	809	KT
Knight of St Patrick	1783*	KP
Knight Grand Cross of the Bath	1725	GCB
Order of Merit	1902	OM
Knight Grand Commander, Star of India	1861	GCSI
Knight Grand Cross, St Michael and St George	1818	GCMG
Knight Grand Commander, Order of the Indian Empire	1878*	GCIE
Crown of India (Ladies)	1878*	CI
Knight Grand Cross, Victorian Order	1896	GCVO
Knight Grand Cross, British Empire	1917	GBE
Companions of Honour	1917	CH
Knight Commander, Bath	1725	KCB
Knight Commander, Star of India	1861	KCSI
Knight Commander, St Michael and St George	1818	KCMG
Knight Commander, Indian Empire	1878*	KCIE
Knight Commander, Victorian Order	1896	KCVO
Knight Commander, British Empire	1917	KBE
Knights Bachelor	**	Kt.
Companion, Bath	1725	CB
Companion, Star of India	1861	CSI
Companion, St Michael and St George	1818	CMG
Companion, Indian Empire	1878*	CIE
Commander, Victorian Order	1896	CVO
Commander, British Empire	1917	CBE
Companion, Distinguished Service Order	1886	DSO

Title	Date of Institution	Abbreviation
Order of the British Empire	1917	OBE
Companion, Imperial Service Order	1902	ISO
Member, British Empire	1917	MBE
Indian Order of Merit	1837*	IOM
Order of British India	1837*	OBI

*Obsolete **Not an order; entitles the recipient to be called 'Sir' but knighthood cannot be passed on to heirs. Awarded for distinguished service.

DECORATIONS FOR GALLANTRY AND DISTINGUISHED SERVICE

Title	Date of Institution	Abbreviation
Victoria Cross	1856	VC
George Cross	1940	GC
Conspicuous Gallantry Cross	1995	CGC
Distinguished Service Order	1886	DSO
Distinguished Service Cross	1901	DSC
Military Cross	1914	MC
Distinguished Flying Cross	1918	DFC
Air Force Cross	1918	AFC
Albert Medal	1866	AM
Distinguished Conduct Medal (army)	1845	DCM
Conspicuous Gallantry Medal (navy & RAF)	1855, 1874	CGM
George Medal	1940	GM
Distinguished Service Medal (navy)	1914	DSM
Military Medal	1916	MM
Distinguished Flying Medal	1918	DFM
British Empire Medal	1917*	BEM

THE ARMED FORCES

The Army

 Field Marshal

 Lieutenant-Colonel
(Lt-Col)

 General (Gen)

 Major (Maj)

 Lieutenant-General
(Lt-Gen)

 Captain (Capt)

 Major-General
(Maj-Gen)

 Lieutenant (Lt)

 Brigadier (Brig)

 Second Lieutenant
(2nd Lt)

 Colonel (Col)

Warrant Officer
Staff Sergeant
Sergeant
Corporal
Lance Corporal
Private

The Royal Navy

 Admiral of the Fleet

 Admiral (Adm)

 Vice-Admiral (Vice-Adm)

 Rear-Admiral (Rear-Adm)

 Commodore (1st and 2nd Class) (Cdre)

 Captain (Capt)

 Commander (Cdr)

 Lieutenant-Commander (Lt-Cdr)

 Lieutenant (Lt)

 Sub-Lieutenant (Sub-Lt)

 Midshipman

Fleet Chief Petty Officer
Chief Petty Officer
Petty Officer
Leading Rating (or Seaman)
Able Rating (or Seaman)
Junior Rating (or Seaman)

The Royal Air Force

  Marshal of the RAF

 Air Chief Marshal

 Air Marshal

 Air Vice-Marshal

 Air Commodore (Air Cdre)

 Group Captain (Gp Capt)

 Wing Commander (Wg Cdr)

 Squadron Leader (Squ Ldr)

 Flight Lieutenant (Flt Lt)

  Flying Officer (FO)

 Pilot Officer (PO)

Acting Pilot Officer
Warrant Officer
Flight Sergeant
Sergeant
Corporal
Junior Technician
Senior Aircraftman
Leading Aircraftman
Aircraftman

THE POLICE

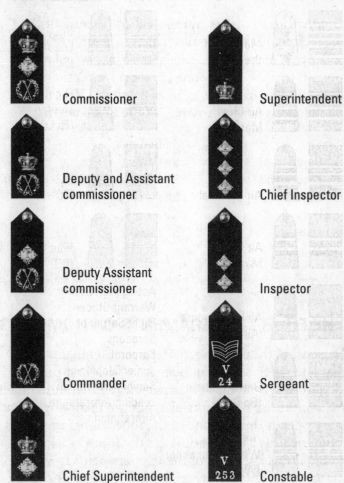

Commissioner

Deputy and Assistant commissioner

Deputy Assistant commissioner

Commander

Chief Superintendent

Superintendent

Chief Inspector

Inspector

Sergeant

Constable

Published by courtesy of the Metropolitan Police Service.

THE KNIGHTS OF THE ROUND TABLE

King Arthur's knights were so-called because of the large, circular table around which they sat and which gave precedence to none, save the king. Popularly thought to have numbered 12, some sources indicate there were many more, even as many as 150. The following list gives the names of the best known:

Sir Kay	Sir Bedivere
Sir Gareth	Sir Gawain
Sir Lancelot du Lac	Sir Tristan de Lyonnais
Sir Galahad	Sir Perceval
Sir Bors	Sir Ector
Sir Tarquin	Sir Lionel
Sir Mordred*	

Mordred was Arthur's son and ultimately responsible for his downfall.

THE FOUR TEMPERAMENTS OR HUMOURS

These were thought to represent the dominant characteristics of human beings, an idea first put forward by Aristotle. It was recognized that individuals are a mixture of all four traits, but the theory held that every person showed one of the four temperaments as a ruling quality. The humours are the four principal bodily fluids and each of the temperaments is characterized by the prevailing influence of one of the humours.

Temperament	Humour	Character
Sanguine	Blood	Cheerfulness
Melancholic	Black bile	Gloominess
Choleric	Yellow bile	Anger
Lethargic or phlegmatic	Phlegm	Apathy

THE SEVEN LIBERAL ARTS

This classification dates from the Middle Ages and was taken to be the basis of secular education.

The Trivium – Logic, Grammar, Rhetoric
The Quadrivium – Arithmetic, Geometry, Astronomy, Music

THE SIX WIVES OF HENRY VIII

1 Catherine of Aragon (divorced)
2 Anne Boleyn (beheaded)
3 Jane Seymour (died)
4 Anne of Cleves (divorced)
5 Catherine Howard (beheaded)
6 Catherine Parr (survived)

THE THREE GRACES (GREEK MYTHOLOGY)

Three sister goddesses, givers of charm and beauty.

Aglaia
Euphrosyne
Thalia; one of the nine Muses

THE NINE MUSES (GREEK MYTHOLOGY)

Nine sister goddesses, daughters of Zeus and Mnemosyne, each regarded as protectress of a different art or science.

Name	Muse of
Calliope	Epic Poetry
Clio	History
Erato	Love Poetry
Euterpe	Lyric Poetry and Music
Melpomene	Tragedy
Polyhymnia	Singing, Mime and Sacred Dance
Terpsichore	Dance and Choral Song
Thalia	Comedy and Pastoral Poetry; one of the Three Graces
Urania	Astronomy

THE LABOURS OF HERCULES

To slay the Nemean lion and bring back its skin
To kill the Lernean Hydra
To catch and retain the Arcadian stag (Ceryneian hind)
To destroy the Erymanthean boar
To cleanse the stables of King Augeas, King of Elis
To destroy the cannibal birds of Lake Stymphalis
To capture the Cretan bull
To catch the horses of the Thracian Diomedes who fed them on
  human flesh
To get possession of the girdle of Hippolyte, Queen of the
  Amazons, and bring it to Admete, daughter of Eurystheus
To capture the oxen of the monster Geryon
To get possession of the apples of the Hesperides
To bring up from the infernal regions the three-headed dog,
  Cerberus

THE SEVEN VIRTUES

Faith	Prudence	Fortitude	Hope
Justice	Temperance	Charity	

The first three are called the Holy Virtues.

THE SEVEN WONDERS OF THE ANCIENT WORLD

Pyramids of Egypt
Hanging Gardens of Babylon
Statue of Zeus at Olympia
Temple of Artemis at Ephesus
Mausoleum of Halicarnassus
Colossus of Rhodes
Pharos (lighthouse) of Alexandria

THE SEVEN SEAS

North Pacific Ocean
South Pacific Ocean
North Atlantic Ocean
South Atlantic Ocean

Arctic Ocean
Antarctic Ocean
Indian Ocean

THE SEVEN DEADLY SINS

Pride
Covetousness
Lust
Envy

Gluttony
Anger
Sloth

THE TWELVE DAYS OF CHRISTMAS

Traditional English carol.

My true love sent to me
A partridge in a pear tree,
Two turtle doves,
Three French hens,
Four calling birds,
Five gold rings,
Six geese a-laying,
Seven swans a-swimming,
Eight maids a-milking,
Nine ladies dancing,
Ten lords a-leaping,
Eleven pipers piping,
Twelve drummers drumming.